# ZERO TO HERO

# ZERO TO HERO

## FROM A BOYS' HOME TO RAF HERO

### PETER W. BODLE FRAeS

FONTHILL

Fonthill Media Limited
www.fonthillmedia.com
office@fonthillmedia.com

First published in the United Kingdom 2014

British Library Cataloguing in Publication Data:
A catalogue record for this book is available from the British Library

ISBN 978-1-78155-303-9

Typeset in 10pt on13pt Sabon Lt Std
Printed and bound by CPI Group (UK) Ltd, Croydon, CR0 4YY

# Contents

# Contents

# Acknowledgements

Because of the nature of Victor's short life, this acknowledgement list is indeed unusually small. There appears to be few people with knowledge of his early days but we have been fortunate that there have been several who had the ability to shed light on this remarkable young man's flying career. I use that last phrase to highlight the fact that his life prior to joining the RAF can almost be thought of as merely waiting time for his big moment to arrive.

I am delighted to acknowledge here the comprehensive and invaluable contribution put into this book by Jean and Steve de Roeck. Jean was Victor's niece, and as such provided the vital link to the other members of Victor's family, and Steve, as an ex-airline Captain, had the base knowledge and understanding to work through vast collections of aircraft orientated paperwork to get the story straight. It is fair to say that without them, this book simply would not have been possible.

Several of Victor's old RAF colleagues have contributed directly and indirectly, none more so than the members of his first crew, Wireless Radio Operator Doug Cole and Bomb-Aimer, Don Caruthers.

Finally, as always, my grateful thanks to my wife Jane, for many hours spent carefully reading through everything from 'provisional notes' through 'first drafts' to the 'positively the last set of corrections', that this book as thrown up over its three years of research and production.

My thanks indeed go to everyone who has helped me reveal this remarkable young man's short but gallant career and put it out in the public domain where it richly deserves to be.

Peter W. Bodle FRAeS
Penryn
March 2014

# Introduction

Over the past ten or twenty years I have had the pleasure of meeting several survivors of Don Bennett's Pathfinder crews, and in many cases, to get to know them well. Regardless of their rank or seniority, one common characteristic that has struck me the most was their genuine modesty and the matter-of-fact attitude they had to the fantastically dangerous job that they did during those dark wartime days. It was also noticeable how they all took what they did for granted. It was simply 'their' role in the war situation, and to a man, they made it clear they would not have swapped it for any other. Understandably I never met Victor Roe, but it appears from what I have learned of him during the years of research for this book, he was very obviously a man out of the same mould.

For over fifty years his story has been collected, pieced together and kept carefully preserved by the family he never knew. In the last decade or so, further fresh information has been unearthed about Victor from a variety of reliable sources, and because of the discovery of the more recent papers, these earlier private archives have been added to in a way that now makes it possible to piece Victor's life story together. Although not as complete as a personal diary, there is now enough information amassed for his story to be published and rightfully take its place amongst the manuscripts of Britain's better-known heroes of the Second World War. He did not believe himself a hero, and apart from colleagues, a few friends and family, no one else knew his story. However, anyone who completed over ninety combat operations as a tail gunner in the Pathfinder Force, or the wider Bomber Command for that matter, is for sure a fully paid up hero in anyone's eyes ... unless of course there is a higher accolade that describes him.

I was delighted to be asked by Victor's family to put this all together in one book and now is the time for the wider world to be made aware of the story of this dedicated young man's short but extraordinary life.

# 1

# A Fegan's Boy

The official paperwork and forms that on 11 January 1943, turned Victor Arthur Roe from a civilian, employed in a reserved occupation, to a member of His Majesty's armed forces would seem innocuous enough at first glance. Some workers in reserved occupations were discouraged from volunteering; others were indeed prohibited by law. It could be argued that Victor was in some ways fortunate to be allowed to even apply for aircrew. Nonetheless he managed it and the standard government, beige coloured forms, letterpress printed on a very poor quality paper, each one separate with a very official title at the top and a unique reference number on the bottom, confirmed that fact. However, once you start to ask searching questions about the background to some of the entries on Victor (Vic) Roe's form, you start to unearth a story that was far from ordinary about a man who was himself, very far from ordinary.

On the first page of form 543, issued from RAF Halton, sometime after Victor's death, the Civil Occupation section contained the words Farm Labourer, from District 168, which was indeed factually true. However digging a little deeper behind that simple statement you would find that in actuality he was one of a unique group of lads who trained as farm workers on a farm named High Horden, in Kent. High Horden was near the village of Goudhurst on the Kent and Sussex border just a few miles from Royal Tunbridge Wells, some twenty miles inland from Hastings. (High Horden is now the site of HM Prison, Blantyre House, having been acquired from the Fegan organisation in 1954). For anyone familiar with the social structure and the devastation wrought by the 1930s depression in that lower working-class section of pre-war Britain, the High Horden address would have signified that Victor Roe was a Fegan Boy. A Fegan Boy was simply a child from a Boys' Home; but that understates the situation by miles.

To begin to understand Victor Roe, it is necessary to look closely at his early years as a child of the Great Depression and from what would today be called a 'dysfunctional family'. Victor's parents Clifford and Laura had a total of ten children between them, including one stepchild, of whom nine survived. They were virtually destitute, despite Clifford's declared trade as a 'Boot Clicker', a well-paid and respected trade also known as a shoe pressman, cutting the shapes of shoe components from the leather hides, in a city full of shoe manufacturers. Early in their lives they had both acquired a lifelong addiction to alcohol which no doubt was the root cause of their downfall. The combination of this lethal mix of poverty and drink was hugely devastating to Victor and all his siblings. It also split the Roe family in further directions as Clifford's and Laura's parents eventually decided they could handle the situation no longer and threw in the towel and disowned them.

Victor was born on Thursday 24 May 1923, at Old Barge Yard, close to the banks of the River Wensum, in the centre of Norwich. As with all the Roe children, by the time he reached three and well before his fourth birthday, the local authority had exercised their responsibility to remove him from his parents' custody, and had made alternative arrangements for his future upbringing. All the Roe offspring started their young lives in the care of one of the Children's Homes, scattered around the city of Norwich. It was not an auspicious start for any of them.

Victor was placed in the care of The Norwich Home in Turner Road, on the western fringes of the city, when he was just three years old. At the appropriate age he started his early education at the Surrey Road Primary School, progressing a few years later to the Nelson Street Senior Boys' School. His father died while he was at the Surrey Road School, and his mother re-married while he was at the Nelson Street School. There is no surviving record to tell us if the young Victor attended either the funeral of his father, or the second marriage of his mother. It is most likely, given the family's severely fractured circumstances that he did not.

Just a few days short of his twelfth birthday, at the behest of the Norwich authorities, he was transferred to Mr Fegan's Home for Boys in Yardley Gobian, near Stony Stratford, in Buckinghamshire. He followed in the footsteps of his older brothers Bert and Wilfred who had passed through the Fegan's system, some three and ten years earlier. It was Thursday 2 May 1935. When he arrived he was instantly confronted with a totally new way of life; that of living as one of a group, within an institution that was run with pretty rigid structures and rules. Fegan's boys were all from homes whose backgrounds, for a variety of reasons, left much to be desired; including some who simply had been abandoned by their parents and whatever family they had. The common thread was that they all needed, or were thought to need, the type of upbringing that the institutional life in a boy's home could bring. Whether this was true or not was never questioned and whether the boy himself had any views on the matter were considered irrelevant, and thus never ever solicited. Although by no means a prison or institution in the penal sense, the only way out of the situation for the boys was to follow the pattern set out by the Fegan Homes' authorities. That way they would progress through the home, on to the organisation's own farm, then onward to the real world, either in this country or as an emigrant to a new life in Canada. The harsh reality of life in those days was that for most of the boys in the Fegan's Homes system, there simply was no obvious alternative.

However, this is jumping the gun somewhat, and for the young Victor Roe, the first days at the Fegan Home at Stony Stratford were the same confusing nightmare that befell all new Fegan boys. It was primarily a combination of being somewhere strange with people he did not know and the instant introduction to a benign but total lack of freedom and the mandatory adherence to a pre-set routine; all things that would of course greatly assist him when he joined the RAF later on in life. As one contemporary of his noted of the system, 'It seemed as if Fegan's now actually owned you'. This contemporary commentator's thoughts then went on to suggest that the RAF basic training period was more like a holiday camp to him when he compared it to the previous rigidity of the all-encompassing Fegan's routine. No doubt, Victor felt much the same.

When Victor awoke every morning at half past six, once his consciousness had registered which day of the week it was, he automatically knew what the routine would be for that day. That meant that he knew what he would be wearing, what he would be doing and in what order, and exactly what meals he would be eating and at what time of day all of these things would happen. This was based on knowledge of the unchanging Fegan's routine, not weekly or monthly or annually … eternally … it was as if set in stone. At Fegan's, the routines never, ever changed. This rigidity of routine seemed to be solely based on the fact that as it had worked for the last decade or more, then no one could see any good reason to alter it. Although it has to be said, that no one actually asked the boys if they had a view on it, or they may well have got some fairly unexpected answers and a rather different perspective on things.

It is also worth noting at this stage that none of the Fegan's boys wore watches, only the masters were allowed that luxury, so the passage of time for the boys at Stony Stratford was solely marked by these rigid timetables. From that point of view, this inflexible system can be seen to hold some merit.

By 06.35 a.m. Victor and all the boys had abandoned their standard issue Fegan nightshirts and having donned part of their day outfit, had trooped to the communal bathroom to have the regulation strip wash. This was followed by another eternal Fegan ritual, the cleanliness inspection. Only after that did they complete the dressing routine by putting on shirts (no boys were ever issued with vests) and if the colder months dictated it, pullovers. Then they all headed off to breakfast, which like all Fegan's meals was rigidly inflexible. Porridge and two thick slices of bread pre-coated with a thin spread of margarine accompanied by a cup of warm cocoa. After this they dispersed to do 'jobs' before finally arriving, via the 'marking off' parade at 09.00 a.m. to the classrooms. Before the parade, beds had all been made, dormitories tidied up, and all other domestic duties completed. On a personal front, boots had to be cleaned and polished, hair combed and a general air of being spruced up and ready for the day was expected to be achieved by all. Then followed, the Fegan's 'marking-off' of all the boys assembled, on to the ubiquitous 'marking off' sheet which was as much an integral part of Fegan's as getting up in the morning and drawing breath. It involved a crocodile of boys walking past a master who was assisted by one of the boys who operated the 'marking off' sheet. As they passed the master each boy shouted his number, and the 'marking off' boy acknowledged his presence by placing a tick in the appropriate line on the sheet. This way the Fegan system was complete for the next few hours, until the next 'marking off' parade dictated that it was all done over again.

In his early years as a junior, Victor would have gone to school for several hours in the morning. Then after dinner (more of which later) the 02.00 p.m. assembly and a further edition of the Fegan 'marking off' ritual would have heralded another few hours session in the classroom. It was all aimed at a very basic education. None of the boys were studying towards the Grammar School exam. As the final destination for all Fegan's boys was deemed to be the farm at Goudhurst, the additional work for the grammar school entrance exam was considered irrelevant and unnecessary. As the years passed and Victor became a senior, he would have progressed to the top form where the headmaster presided over the classroom and imparted the knowledge that Fegan's felt the boys would need for their eventual progress to the Goudhurst farm and a few years after that, to the outside world.

But first would come the transitional period in Victor's life when, as a senior, he became a 'working boy'. In the simple philosophy of the institution, after a boy had been taught all that he needed to know in scholastic matters, the thought was that he needed to be taught how to work. What simpler way to achieve this, than actually to put him to work in the school, doing all the basic tasks needed to keep such a large operation running? Twelve to fifteen working boys were involved at any one time and they held those positions for about eight months before heading off to work on the farm and to receive further instruction on the more practical aspects of working life. Victor's options as a working boy would have been one of the following—a kitchen boy, a boiler boy, a coke boy, a chicken and pig boy, a gardening boy, or lastly a general boy, doing the myriad of tidying up tasks not already accomplished by those miscreants on punishment duties. When we say options we are of course not referring to the boys' own choices, rather the options that the master had for selecting the duties any boy could be allotted. One duty that seemed to be universal and involved each and every boy at the Stony Stratford home was the ritual of sweeping the playground, known to all as 'The Parade'. Never a day, save Sundays of course, went by when an already spotlessly clean playground was not swept yet again to within an inch of its life by the 'duty sweepers'. There was also the need to have a working boy available to serve the masters their meals and to do the washing up after they had eaten. Whatever duty Victor had been allocated, like almost all Fagan functions, it stayed the same every day for the entire duration of his eight months 'working boy' secondment.

Meals were adequate if completely unimaginative, and as with all Fegan's boys activities, routine and entirely predictable. On Mondays Victor would have rissoles, Tuesday it was stew, and Wednesday would provide him with Pease Pudding and so on through the remainder of the week. The following week would be exactly the same. Desserts were also similarly regimented but to everyone's delight, occasionally bore a slight resemblance to food available in the outside world, even if the custard and treacle were always somewhat thinner and runnier than the manufacturers ever imagined could be achieved with their products. At this point it is well worth mentioning that the standard drink for the boys at Fegan's was cocoa. Not quite the same flavoursome chocolate drink that we know it as today, although the name is the same. It was said that it was usually served lukewarm and had a very much an acquired taste, although no written record appears to exist to detail the precise flavour of the liquid. Some of Victor's contemporaries have suggested that there were in fact no words yet invented in the English language that were fully able to describe it.

Victor's weekends were inevitably taken up with sports and exercise. The Fegan's regime put great store in health and fitness and were very keen to field teams in as many popular sports as possible and compete against other local schools and organisations. It was almost certain that it was about this time that his love of playing football really took hold, and became a passion that remained with him for the rest of his life. On other occasions, organised (escorted) walks were undertaken once or twice a month to get the boys out of the confines of the home, even if only for an hour or two. One of the places more popular with the boys was an area to the East of Stoney Stratford where the Grand Union Canal and River Great Ouse cross, via an aqueduct.

Evening and winter pursuits included chess and draughts, though surprisingly reading was not a particularly popular pastime, mainly because there were so few quiet places for boys to sit and read by themselves. As you can imagine, any building, however large, when occupied by dozens of healthy, lively young boys, is always going to be alive with noise, chatter and laughter. Whilst I'm not sure how many boys would have liked to slip quietly away on their own to some quiet corner to read, as the greater majority were convinced that they already did sufficient reading for any young lad of their age. The reading they were confronted with during their normal daytime lessons was considered by most to be sufficient and more of the same was simply not needed; although for some, an occasional moment of peace and quiet would probably have been appreciated.

All too soon it was Victor's turn to be prepared for the next stage of the Fegan training and on 20 April 1938 he moved out of Stony Stratford and like thousands before him, was sent to work on the organisation's farm at Goudhurst. This was a completely new experience for him. It had a more relaxed and adult atmosphere, his pocket money increased and above all, the jobs they were given to do all had a meaning. The cows had to be fed and milked, and all animals had to be tended regardless of time, date and weather and at the appropriate time of the year the crops had to be harvested. To Victor, it all now stared to fit together.

It probably also makes sense to start with the Farm Timetable of activity that Victor inherited from his predecessors, and indeed a few years later passed on completely unchanged to his young successors.

| 05.00 | Call for boys cleaning cows |
|-------|------------------------------|
| 05.15 | Call for boys milking cows |
| 05.30 | Call for boys tending horses, on kitchen duties and in the boiler house |
| 06.30 | Call for the remainder of the boys |
| 07.00 | Breakfast |
| 08.00 | Parade in Barnyard for morning duty allocation |
| 12.00 | Lunch |
| 13.00 | Parade in Barnyard for afternoon duty allocation |
| 17.00 | Tea |
| 18.00 | Recreation time |
| 20.30 | Supper |
| 21.00 | Bed and lights out |

This was the pattern of life for Victor and the fifty to one hundred boys who were resident at the farm with him at any one time during his stay. Saturdays and Sundays made little difference to those boys whose tasks involved the welfare of the animals, but Sunday was, for all of them, a major psychological change. Sunday was the day they all got to wear long trousers. For the remainder of the working week, and through all their days at the home, before they were seconded to the farm, all Fegan's boys, always wore shorts, and black boots, there were no exceptions. However, long trousers on Sundays at the farm elevated them to the status of 'normal' humans. In their eyes, that was progress.

The one thing that did not progress or ever change at the farm was the Fegan's adherence to a menu that was set in stone. There appears to be no record if it was the exact same menu they had at the school at Stony Stratford, but once again the system had decreed that whatever the boys ate for dinner on their first Monday at High Horden, it could be guaranteed that they would have the very same meal on their last Monday, some three years later. Not only that, they would have had an identical meal on all 154 Mondays in between, unless of course Christmas Day happened to have fallen on a Monday in one of their three years of attendance. That was the one and only variation to the rule.

When it came to the work schedule, there were also no exceptions to the proven Fegan system of starting at the bottom and working your way up, year by year. All newcomers to the farm were introduced to its workings via cleaning duties and the more general farming activities as muck spreading, fetching, carrying and yet again, more cleaning. Needless to say the only time that the schedule was officially abandoned in any way was during the harvest period when a more 'all hands on deck' approach was used, as of course was customary throughout the rest of the farming community. Harvest was the time in the High Horden calendar, when every boy and every master was called in to process the crops through the system. In those pre-combine-harvester days, the culmination of the whole cereal growing process, the threshing of the harvest, was extremely hot, dusty, noisy and incredibly labour intensive and it would not be unusual to need fifteen to twenty people to keep the flow of cereal production running smoothly.

During his stay at the farm, Victor and the other lads in his intake were allocated the jobs according to the well-established Fegan roster, and as such he took his turn at all the farming duties needed to help keep High Horden running efficiently. Most were fun in some way or other, but understandably they were all 'men's' jobs, as the lads, in addition to learning practical skills, were really being toughened up. They were being taught to work hard and be useful members of the society they were due to join in a few years' time when their time at Goudhurst was completed. However amongst the really enjoyable duties there were some skills they would have rather preferred to avoid learning. Universally disliked was the messy but necessary treatment of the fruit trees when the post-harvest process of spraying the trees with their winter wash of Tar-Oil was carried out. It was hot, sticky, smelly and a generally unpleasant experience. To most lads the tractor driving duties were pretty much at the top of the list of things they preferred to do and for most of them, working with the animals was running it a close second on the favourites list.

As with his time at the home at Stony Stratford, Victor found that the High Horden boys and their mentors were very keen on sports and fielded teams in both football and cricket, to take on sides from other nearby senior schools and the pub and village leagues from around the local neighbourhood. During the summer months swimming was a very well appreciated activity as part of both the fitness curriculum and also as a leisure time pursuit for the boys. It appeared to be an area of activity that encouraged a somewhat freer approach than other more formal parts of the Fegan System, thus a quick dip in the pool after dinner and before afternoon work, while not on the schedule, was never frowned upon. It must be remembered of course that the big Swimming Gala Day was one of the highlights of the High Horden year.

The other continuing practice that had obviously followed them was the regulation attendance for Sunday worship in the farm chapel. Unsurprisingly by now, along with most of the other senior lads, Victor's voice had broken, and contemporary writings have complemented the rich, deep tones of the religious singing that were heard emanating from the High Horden chapel on a weekly basis.

The other lasting lesson in life that was instilled into the boys was the allocation and management of pocket money (wages). It ranged from two shillings and sixpence per week for a senior boy, down to four pence a week for a fourth grade junior. Grading was calculated through a combination of factors including age, experience and the ability to not do anything to incur the wrath of one of the masters. Every master had the power to dock a percentage of a boy's wages for serious misdemeanours, or in the harshest of cases, cancel it altogether for that week. Needless to say Victor and his colleagues were more than keen not to cause offence. However, if offence was inevitable, they learned to be adept at hiding as many of the other current infringements as possible from their eagle-eyed mentors, thus keeping their personal cash flow at the maximum allowed. For Victor and his fellow Farm Boys, it was a hard lesson but one that they all learned quickly and did well to remember.

After three or more years 'work experience' at High Horden, The Fegan system deemed Victor Roe was fully trained and ready to face the world and take his rightful place in society. On Sunday 2 August Victor had his last ever Fegan's breakfast, collected his few personal possessions together and headed off on the short walk to his new home and job on the Bernstein Estate at Copping Farm, just couple of miles to the north west of Leigh, near Tonbridge in Kent. Here he began his adult working life and although the wage packet was still somewhat modest, he started to earn 'real' money and further consolidate his knowledge of the farming industry. He remained with the Bernstein organisation at Copping Farm until finally enlisting in the RAF some seventeen months later.

Unsurprisingly, all this in itself registered little outside Victor's own small circle of friends. By then the rest of the world had something far more urgent weighing on its mind at that point in time … the rise of the ultra-fanatical, right wing, Germany Nazi party, led by Adolf Hitler and with it the impending World War that Hitler and his cohorts were determined to inflict on Europe and the rest of the world. Although he did not know it at the time, it was also the event that would also keep the young Victor fully occupied for the remainder of his life.

# 2

# How Things Were

Ninety years or so on from the birth of Victor's generation, it is probably worth explaining some of the social and economic differences that were governing the lives of the majority of the British population around that time. The 1920s world was vastly different from the post-2000 era that would cover most people's experiences. The social structure, though far less inflexible and strict than anything that was in place before the First World War, was certainly far more rigid, structured and harsher, than the world we know today. The British class system still reigned supreme.

At the top of the social scale there were the landed gentry who in general terms did not work and generally derived a plentiful income from their vast family estates and investments. Next in line there were the factory owners and the owners of the smaller estates and large farms, who probably worked a little, but relied almost entirely on the labour of others to earn them their fortunes. Of course there was, as ever, the layer of the professional classes of doctors, lawyers, accountants and the like, who by and large did pretty well for themselves and held a prominent position in society. Then slightly further down the scale there were 'trade'; people who we today would classify as shopkeepers and merchants. Again their lives were quite reasonable by the standards of the day and they had a generally comfortable existence but usually had to work quite hard and sometimes for long hours to earn their wages. Those in the military also did well, but it too had a structure that also closely reflected the social streams in the civilian world and needless to say, the better the rank, the better the pay, the uniform and the conditions. Somewhere about here in the 'pecking order' of society came the tradesmen, who generally survived and never starved as their skills were usually in great demand. However below this line in society, life was starting to become a struggle. Un-skilled workers, labourers, itinerant workers and casual and seasonal labourers were always pretty much on the breadline and wondering where the next pay cheque was coming from. Beneath that life for the unemployed was at best rough, at worst, truly hell on earth.

A small flavour of the 'then and now' comparisons are listed below. Victor would have been reasonably familiar with many of the 1925 to 1935 prices. (Here quoted in the values of the day. Old Pence {d} of which there were 12 in one Shilling {written 1/-},

30 in the Half Crown {written 2/6} and 240 in the Pound Sterling {written £1}). The monetary system he would have been taught at school, but he would certainly not have been too familiar with the idea of having very much of it or of being able to purchase any of the items in question ... most of them were way beyond his reach and that of the people sharing his section of English society. In his part of the world in the early to mid thirties, it was all strictly window shopping or at best a penny or two for sweets. Although somewhat looser than it was before the start of the First World War, some twenty-five years earlier, the long established British class structure still ruled supreme and maintained an unshakable stranglehold on all aspects of everyday society.

## A Generality of 1925–1935 Prices

| | |
|---|---|
| Two-Bedroom House | £350 |
| Gallon of Petrol | 1/6 (18*d*) |
| Family Car | £120 |
| Pint of Beer | 2*d* |
| Postage Stamp | 1*d* or 2*d* |
| Pint of Milk | 3*d* |
| Newspaper | 2*d* |
| 5 Cigarettes | 1*d* |

Weekly Earnings

| | |
|---|---|
| Labourer | £4.10/- |
| Miner | £6 to £3.19/- |
| Skilled Tradesman | £5 |
| Average wage 1930 | £3.19/- |
| Average wage 1935 | £3.14/6 |

Beneath this layer of self-sufficient and semi self-sufficient members of society, there were of course the underclasses that relied totally on Church, State and Charitable Institutions to contribute to their very survival. Within these lower social stratas of pre Second World War Britain the dividing lines were frequently blurred and people and families could float between being simply poor to destitute very quickly. The route back was possible, but usually quite hard, or in need of a stroke of luck. It was a very uncertain existence. Finally, as in any society, there were also the remaining few who survived by operating the wrong side of the law, using robbery, pickpocketing and begging, and anything and everything else in between to obtain enough money to live.

Houses, flats and other places to live for the working classes were nowhere near as plentiful as they are now, and many of the poorer families lived in just one or two rooms in a tenement building that might easily house dozens of families or more, at any one time. The standard of these dwellings was pretty bad at best, and verged on appalling for the greater majority. They were frequently without gas, electricity, running water or even basic sanitation. A labourer's wages were usually pretty dire, so what public transport was available was not usually affordable to those who needed most to keep in employment. The lucky few may have had an old bicycle to ride to work, the greater majority simply walked. A few enlightened companies may have provided transport for key workers, but this would have been a very rare situation indeed, and primarily for the company's benefit.

Food was always disproportionally expensive to those on low wages and welfare, and thus the staple diet of many of the lower classes was simply inadequate to maintain health and fitness. Death by malnutrition and its various associated illnesses was commonplace, and as always, the children were the most vulnerable. In a perverse way, it could be argued that the early placement of Victor and the remainder of the Roe children into care homes at a very young age may well have ensured their survival.

It is also worth remembering that health and hygiene amongst the lower echelons of British society in those days left a lot to be desired. Many workers' homes were even below the low standards of the day and for example did not yet having cold running water, toilets, bathrooms or heating. Tin baths in the scullery or behind a screen in one of the rooms was usually the best that there was for a 'quick cleanse'. More often than not it was a wash in the sink, or no wash at all for many a day. Other than that it was an occasional trip to the town's public baths, where hard earned money was spent to get hot water and soap. Communal outside toilets frequently served several families, and as such were not always the most salubrious or hygienic of places. Strangely by being removed from this environment into care, Victor would have moved into a world where a weekly warm bath and somewhat better sanitary arrangements would have been the norm. This was because such facilities were the minimum requirement imposed by the Local Authority who had the legal responsibility for the children's health and welfare. Such legal requirements did not fall on private landlords or even on the builders providing New Build domestic houses, although inside bathrooms and toilets were starting to become more popular and a fairly regular feature of new houses for sale.

Employers in those days rarely addressed these sorts of problems either. Most work places, factories and even some smaller shops rarely provided any washing facilities for their staff and workers; who inevitably went home to wash, still dirty, dusty and smelly from long hours labouring at their chosen profession. One can but imagine the plethora of smells permeating the streets when walking home in the company of those who had spent all day working in an onion processing plant, a leather tannery, a fish processing plant or even the local sewage works.

Victor's institutional childhood would have ensured that he had always had clothes to wear and shoes on his feet, or sturdy boots, to be more precise. The lower Working Class strata of society surrounding Victor was known for the use of strong hard wearing clothes that in theory at least were made to last forever. Footwear would usually be tough, black boots, generally with the soles reinforced by the addition of hard wearing steel 'Hob Nails' and crescent shaped steel inserts in the heels to make them last. Clothes for the lower orders had no need of style, refinement or comfort. Those finer qualities were reserved solely for the clothes for the gentry where there was no fear that they would get damaged by anything resembling work! The quality of material used for clothing went from refined to rough as it filtered downward throughout the class structure. Likewise footwear followed the same pattern going from shoes that were stylish, comfortable and light down through society to rough, sturdy, black boots for those towards the lower end of the social order. However at the very bottom, the children particularly, were known to go barefoot for most of their early lives. A second-hand pair of school shoes may well have been their first experience of genuine footwear and in many cases the socks to go with them could well have been an afterthought as they were seen by some families as a bit of a luxury.

In a society where the survival of the poorer was not guaranteed, and an early demise through malnutrition, a lack of medical care or the lack of decent shelter was not that uncommon, it is hardly surprising that things like holidays, Christmas and birthday presents, rarely featured in the lives of the children in the care of local authorities. Those everyday things taken for granted in the twenty-first century, such as a trip to the cinemas (black and white in those days), a trip to the zoo, or to the seaside, were totally out of their reach. The best that they might hope to achieve was a wander through the local fairground if it was pitched in a field within walking distance of the home. It would also be just that, a wander through, with wide eyes taking in the sights. The prospect of having any money to spend on rides or stalls was highly unlikely, unless of course they were lucky enough to have found the odd coin that had been dropped by an earlier visitor.

Children from the working class families would not have had high expectations for Christmas and birthday presents. A Christmas meal that was somewhat 'better' than usual would be the highlight of the day. Often a single toy, frequently home-made, would have been all a child would have wished for, and if accompanied by an orange and a handful of sweets or even a small chocolate bar, would have fulfilled all their hopes and dreams. The days of children having a multitude of presents to mark such an occasion were still many years in the future, and not something Victor would have been familiar with. It would take the social revolution that accompanied the Second World War and its aftermath before the poorer members of British society were to get a fairer share of the nation's wealth.

# 3

# *The RAF*

By 11 January 1943, Victor had signed all the appropriate forms and was heading north to No. 1 ACRC (Air Crew Reception Centre) at the famous Lord's Cricket Ground in the heart of London, and from there to 14 Initial Training Wing (14 ITW) for his basic training as RAF Aircrew. A previously unsung, but incredibly distinguished career had just got under way; but even to get that far had not all been plain sailing. There are no surviving records of Victor's thought processes prior to his joining the RAF. Whether he ever considered the Army or Navy an alternative choice for his war service is not known. Obviously due to his background, there were no deep-seated family or other tangible connections with any of the services. From this we have to assume that Victor's thought processes and choice were similar to many young men of that time. Where can I serve best and what would I prefer to do, given the choice? We do know that some seven months after leaving Fegan's he applied to the RAF for an aircrew posting and was turned down for reasons that were not totally clear in Victor's records. But he was single minded and extremely determined and had absolutely no intention of taking 'no' for an answer. So he tried again. This time, just nine months after his first rejection he re-applied and was passed A1 and immediately recommended for aircrew training.

Having passed the written tests and the several long days of physical and medical tests, in a totally satisfactory manner, he was then ushered along the corridor for the final hurdle prior to becoming selected for aircrew, the personal interview. As these were always a private affair between the candidates and the interview board, usually comprising of three RAF recruitment specialists, no details are known of what passed behind those closed door. Suffice to say that when he emerged, Victor had impressed enough and given a sufficient number of right answers to get signed on to train as a Rear Gunner, in the heavy bomber fleet of Bomber Command. He was selected for RAF Aircrew, not a half shabby result for a farmer's lad from a boys' home.

The Rear Gunners, or 'Tail End Charlie', as they were affectionately known, had the important, if sometimes unenviable task, of protecting the rear of the plane from fighter attack. The rear of any bomber was the favourite attack quarter for many of the Luftwaffe's fighter pilots, as they believed it gave them a far better advantage than attacking from any other angle; this, despite the fact that the rear gunner had a considerable arc of fire, often around a full 120 degrees swing. An approach from any other direction was believed to make any close-in attack a far more risky business. The preferred Luftwaffe thinking appeared to be that two fighters attacking together about ninety degrees apart was probably the safest plan and the one most likely to deliver success. It was a great idea on paper, but one rarely possible to execute in the heat of battle, especially at night. Many Luftwaffe pilots preferred to rely solely on the power of the longer range 20 mm cannons that were the standard weaponry in the German night-fighter arsenal at the time.

On Monday 11 January 1943, Victor arrived at RAF Bridlington, home of 14 ITW. It was there that he was to undertake his six weeks Induction Training. Settling in would probably have been fairly easy for him, with his recent past experiences of communal living. New recruits were generally housed four to a room and twenty-four to a house or billet. He was again back to being part of a team. However, the primary non-team members of 14 ITW who dominated the new recruits' lives for those few weeks were the RAF Corporal PT Instructors. They put the raw newcomers through their paces (some would prefer to call it hell) with PT, drill, long runs and that long time military favourite, learning to march. It was not unusual for the PT session to last from sunrise to sunset, or even longer. Victor's love of sport and his long attachment to playing football served him well, while others in his intake suffered mightily from leading a soft life in Civvie Street, prior to offering their services to King and Country.

However regular and unimaginative the Fegan's meals may have been, they were a sizable cut above those served up to the new RAF recruits in both the flavour and quality departments. It was assumed by the originators of the RAF Initial Training programme that hungry teenage boys would eat anything, and it was fair to say after the first day or two, they did. It was that or go hungry. Recruits ate in a production line of tired, hungry lads sitting along tables in rows of dozens that spread away into the distance in either direction. They always ate with cold wet cutlery, recently washed and hosed down from the previous sitting that had finished their meal just a few minutes earlier. During all the years of the war, it never ever varied.

At this stage of training their uniforms had arrived and the adaptation of the Military 'one size fits all' gents' outfitting system was sorted, shuffled and swapped around so that after a day or two, most of the recruits had a uniform that pretty much fitted. By 1943 the MOD/RAF procurement and stores system was running almost smoothly; this was much, much better than it did for Victor's predecessors, for whom in 1941 and 1942 it was not unknown for it to take the whole of the six-week period of basic training for some of the chaps to get their complete uniform issued. It was often said it then took them a further six weeks to make it all fit!

Victor's previous life in institutions had prepared him well and helped him ease gently into RAF life, whereas many other recruits in his intake from a more normal family background found the going very tough indeed. He already knew how to polish his shoes, how to fold his clothes and how to avoid the inspecting eye of anyone in authority. At the end of his basic training period he could also claim to understand 'military speak', he could march, he could salute and stand to attention but most importantly, he could spot an officer at over one hundred paces. He had indeed become an Airman. He was then sent with the majority of his intake of would-be air-gunners, to RAF Bridgenorth in Shropshire to learn the rudiments of gunnery at the Elementary Air Gunners' School. Having got that far and having continued to pass all the tests thrown at him, the next phase of the RAF's training programme was to enable Victor to get his hands on the guns of a real live Lancaster Bomber. This phase of the training would however take somewhat longer than those before it, yet in many ways be a far more pleasant and satisfying experience.

No. 8 Bombing and Air Gunnery School at RAF Evanton, on the shores of the Cromarty Firth near Inverness was Victor's next stop in his RAF career. It was one of the RAF's main Air Gunnery Training establishments and was shared with the Royal Navy, to whom it was known as HMS *Fieldfair*. Here he was taught to shoot and to look after his weaponry. This included how to clear any machine blockage and how to make repairs in mid-air and as many other aspects of gunnery that the RAF felt they could pass on to him in the few short weeks he was available to them. With the RAF's love of acronyms, by the time he left Evanton he had to be proficient at, FRBT, FRRS, FRUT, FRAT and FRQT! These strange sounding exercises broke down as follows.

| | |
|---|---|
| Free gun abeam test | FRBT |
| Free gun relative speed test | FRRS |
| Free gun under tail test | FRUT |
| Free gun astern test | FRAT |
| Free gun Quarter Cross over | FRQT |

But that is all several weeks in the future as Victor arrived with his single kit bag at the gates of RAF Evanton and reported to the Orderly Room. The new intake was grouped into sixes for the training which was scheduled to take six weeks. It was here that Victor started to feel that he had made it. Flying Kit was issued and along with it came the white flash for his cap that indicated he was an RAF Gunnery Trainee. As with all his intake, he gained his first promotion and became an LAC (Leading Aircraftsman) which entitled him to wear the propeller badge that came with the kit. In some ways the white flash became the most prestigious symbol for the trainees as it was recognised off camp. This meant in the local pubs, Victor was recognised as a chap that was training to fight for King and Country. Many civilians were of a mind to buy trainees a pint and to wish them luck. It was a much appreciated bonus that came with the territory.

Soon all the aircrew trainees came down to earth with a bit of a bump when they realised that as well as practising for their chosen combat role, they were all expected to take turns in such delightful military tasks as guard duty, cleaning coal buckets and general sweeping up. Coupled with these 'domestic' tasks there was of course still the obligatory PT, Marching and Drill, activities much cherished by those with any authority over young military recruits.

Despite signing on as an Air Gunner, it was quite some time before Victor or any of his intake were allowed to get their hands on a real live gun. Prior to that magic moment they had hours of classroom theory to attend, learn and absorb... in some cases almost to the point of knowing it backwards as well as forward. They followed a curriculum that included Navigation, Aircraft Recognition, Map Reading, Maths and a good healthy grounding on RAF Law and Administration. Only after that did the course start to take them anywhere near the Gunnery side of the RAF.

Firstly they were shown a selection of training films, imaginatively titled *RAF Gun Turret Drill 1/7*, *RAF Gun Turret Drill 2/7*, through to *RAF Gun Turret Drill 7/7*. All excellent instructional material, even if the titles were somewhat less than riveting! During the same few weeks they had to learn the pyrotechnics used by both the RAF and the enemy, and also which types of armament to use with the various different weapon systems they were most likely to encounter. It was an incredibly busy and intense six weeks, just as the Intake Officer had promised.

Initially the practical training phase of the course started on the ground in the specially designed and constructed Training Huts. Both of the two main types of gun turret manufactured by Boulton and Paul and Frazer-Nash featured in Victor's training and each recruit was expected to be proficient on both sets of kit, regardless of his final posting. Compared to electronic simulators of the late twentieth century these training systems were primitive—but extremely useful, nonetheless. In each of the huts one of the turrets was located opposite a curved wall that formed the target screen. On to that screen was projected a film of aerial warfare with several 'enemy' planes repeatedly attacking and/or passing close to the trainees position. This was accompanied by the background noise of bomber engines screaming and the unmistakable sharp, staccato foreground rattle of gunfire. A light point was then projected on to this moving backdrop as the trainee's target.

This was obviously the fun part, but unfortunately due to the pressures within Bomber Command, no trainee could ever expect to stay in the simulator hut for as long as they really wanted to, so further theory and practical lessons were included in the curriculum to help fill their days. Other huts on site were equipped with aircraft recognition equipment where, after several hours of intensive learning and testing, the instructors were ever hopeful that the new boys would aim at the 'bad guys' and leave 'the good guys' alone. This training was accomplished by displaying photos and silhouettes of planes from several different angles. Then the same aircraft was projected on to screens at different sizes to give the new gunners the opportunity to learn how to estimate the distance between themselves and their targets. Simply put, as Victor was told:

Fire when they are too far away and all you do is make a lot of noise, feel better yourself and waste a lot of bullets; leave it too late and you may well have missed your one and only chance to shoot down your man, thus leaving your plane vulnerable and you and your whole crew in a very dangerous position.

At about this time, the majority of the training syllabus became the warning section. Don't 'hosepipe' the enemy, i.e. don't wave the gun back and forth with a stream of bullets heading off in the enemy's general direction. You probably would not hit anything, and would be using bullets at the rate of ten every second. With an effective range of only 400 yards it was a noisy waste of time and resources. Don't forget to take into account 'bullet drop' ... don't forget the 'deflection' of your target; i.e. shoot where the enemy plane will be when your bullets arrive, not where it was when you squeezed the trigger. There was a lot for Victor and his intake of new boys to learn and practise.

It was probably true to say that for every 'don't', there were usually three or four 'do's' all designed to make sure that the 'don't', didn't.

On slightly more practical matters, they were trained to strip and reassemble any of their guns in two minutes flat. Just to add to the fun, in the final test this Machiavellian piece of RAF training had to be done blindfolded; a sensible requirement as it so happened, as it was very likely that this procedure would have to be done mid raid, in the dead of night, under considerable pressure. Obviously to achieve this required level of professionalism, the trainees learned and then practised this procedure numerous times during their six weeks training. The RAF theory was that when they needed to do this 'for real' it had to be a totally automatic procedure.

On the first day at RAF Evanton, Victor had been told during the initial briefing that it was to be an intensive training course. As he once again found out, the Intake Officer had not been exaggerating.

One of the next buildings across the station was the Turret Training Hut. This contained examples of every gun turret in use within the RAF. For the Bomber Intake the breakdown of the range was; the nose turret, the upper turret, the ventral turret and of course Victor's eventual home, the tail turret. Each student was required to learn all there was to know about each of the turrets and all the idiosyncrasies of the equipment provided by the three manufacturers. Frazer-Nash, Boulton Paul and Bristol all supplied their own variations on a theme, some being hydraulically operated, others electrically powered, in each case the power being derived from the plane's own engines. The days of all planes having the luxury of separate auxiliary power units had yet to arrive.

As with all Gunnery Schools, RAF Evanton had a live firing range attached to it. Live firing ranges were designed to give the students a feel for their turrets under real conditions of sound, smell and all the other aspects of their job that the Training Huts could not. Turrets were usually mounted on old bomb trailers and the wooden target aircraft, surprisingly not always shaped or painted like German fighters, were on rail bogies that traversed in front of the trainee at speeds chosen by the instructors. Their turrets were powered by small engines that provided the students' environment with realistic vibrations and recoil reactions from the guns as they fired at the passing targets.

Then several weeks into the course came Victor's big day. Along with half a dozen equally eager would-be gunners, he donned his new flying gear and headed out to a rather tired looking Armstrong-Whitworth Whitley to begin his air-to-air training. As he would need something airborne to shoot at, the RAF Drogue Towing Unit attached to RAF Evanton stepped up to provide the answer. This unit had use of several aircraft to take Victor's target drogue airborne, and for the majority of such towing units the Hawker Henley, Fairy Battle and Westland Lysander were the main planes of choice. The drogue was towed behind the tow plane by a wire approximately 1,200-feet long, and the target flag (some 12 feet by 60 feet or 5.6 m by 28 m) on another wire a further 2,200 feet behind that; thus giving the tow plane pilot a sporting chance of survival with the new boys as they got their eyes zoned in and their aims perfected. Those same new boys in the Whitley had been allocated ammunition which was coated with a colored wax. Thus the post-exercise examination of the target flag could reveal the success, or lack of it for each of the trainees, though it is understood that not all the instructors trusted this system that much. Many professed to prefer their own judgment based on many years' experience. Similar air-to-ground exercises were conducted a short way along the Cromarty Firth coast, with the targets either located on the foreshore or on small rafts a few yards out to sea. As well as the marker colours on the ammunition, all training guns were fixed with cine cameras, thus both students and instructors were able to monitor the trainees' progress and correct deficiencies as the course progressed as obviously this was much more preferable to a single pass/fail test after months of expensive training.

However, plotting the success of the students, or otherwise is again stepping a little out of sequence. Victor and his five colleagues were now ready to clamber aboard their Whitley carrying their personal ammunition belts and hopefully have the chance to get some real live Air Gunner time in their logbooks. These ammo belts had all been previously loaded by the trainees themselves; four wax coloured rounds and one tracer, four more with coloured wax and another tracer and so on. Thus if in the course of the exercise they had a stoppage, then they lost marks, as the whole gunnery exercise was then totally down to them ... there was no-one they could blame but themselves if it all came to a spine shuddering halt. Usually they were allocated 100 rounds, sometimes 200, rarely more. In this manner the air-to-air training continued apace, weather permitting, as RAF Evanton was located in the north of Scotland and being very close to the sea, was frequently subject to sea mists. Victor and his fellow students would take it in turns to operate the fixed forward guns in the nose turret and then clamber through to the tail and practise with the Frazer-Nash turret at the rear. As a matter of economics, only one gun at a time of the four available was permitted to each student. 'There's a war on don't you know?' was the often used catch phrase of the day. Victor and his chums were certainly well aware of that every time they put on their uniform, put on their flying suits or clambered into their Whitley. They had little time to talk of anything else.

After several weeks of this, the new recruits were old hands at Gunnery, each having logged something in the order of fifteen to sixteen hours airborne in their shiny new logbooks all of which had now been duly signed off on behalf of Evanton's Senior Training Officer. Next they were all ushered into the exam rooms where they were given papers and tasked to prove they had remembered most of what they had been shown. Once successfully over their final hurdle, the magic word 'Pass' was scribed by the examiner after the Hours Flown entry and the coveted Air Gunners Wings with AG emblazoned in its centre were presented at the intake's passing out parade. Much sewing on of badges occurred that evening before they set off for the obligatory celebration drink. Along with 'Pass' in their logbook, on the page marked Results Of Ab-Initio Courses and Remarks, came the course numbers indicating quite how good they really were as gunners. Victor's were very good. He was a natural.

Stature-wise Victor was not a tall lad and was of slim build, so according to the RAF way of thinking, he was ideally suited to the rear turret of an Avro Lancaster Bomber. Unsurprisingly Victor shared their assessment. Thus pupil and masters were all extremely happy with the selection. But first there was a little matter of gaining some valuable operational experience in the ubiquitous Vickers Wellington. He had achieved his goal; he was off to an Operational Training Unit, 20 OTU at RAF Lossiemouth, and he had been promoted to Sergeant to be sent on his way. This was much more like it!

RAF Lossiemouth, with its traditional wide concrete runways, was a mere forty miles to the south east of Evanton on the opposite shore of the Cromarty Firth. It was just a short truck ride for the Evanton trainees to their new home, and because the airfields were so close together around the mouth of the same river, it was still familiar territory for them on the next phase of their training on the twin engine Wellington medium bomber. Once again it was a six-week course. Training on type in less than six months from putting on his fist RAF uniform was just the thing young Victor was hoping for, and the sight of a long row of Wellingtons parked ready for use, did nothing to curb his enthusiasm.

RAF Lossiemouth (or Lossie as it was frequently shortened to) was built during 1938 and 1939 and handed over to the RAF the moment it was finished. It was pretty much the standard RAF Class A bomber airfield with all that that entailed both good and bad. The accommodation huts were built to house some forty airmen at a time, and unlike previous RAF facilities Victor had encountered, Lossiemouth billets had predominantly single beds rather than two tier bunks. That was the good bit, the not so good part was the fact that the beds were only two foot wide and the somewhat thin mattress was made up of three separate sections, nicknamed 'biscuits', for obvious reasons. The other downside to the station was the fact that the water heating system was not up to the demand. Between ten o'clock at night and five o'clock the following morning, the ablution blocks located between the billets pumped out delightful quantities of hot water. In the daytime between five o'clock and ten o'clock the demand was such that hot and cold water taps invariably both produced cold. Also on the plus side of things, each of the Accommodation Blocks was equipped with two pot belly stoves, one at either end of the hut. This layout giving a much better chance of a little warmth filtering around the hut, rather than the more traditionally encountered 'one stove per hut' allocation usually favoured by the military; a unique allocation that actually enabled the stove itself to glow red hot, yet still allowed the greater majority of the hut to freeze during the worst of the British winter weather.

Meals at RAF Lossiemouth were generally standard wartime RAF fare. As one contemporary of Victor's was heard to remark ... there were always two choices. Take it or leave it. Breakfast was always porridge made with water and powdered milk, and was generally served in the mess between six and 8 o'clock. It was invariably accompanied by bread and butter and jam, though many would argue the butter allocation per person had little to do with the size of even a single slice of the bread provided. All this was washed down with unlimited mugs of military issue, hot, weak tea. Dinners were much the same as meals at other training units, except this time; there was some attempt at cooking it properly and retaining some of the inherent flavours.

Now, as bona fide aircrew, Victor's main task at Lossiemouth was of course to join up with his first real crew and to practise with them to help turn a group of newcomers into a compact fighting unit, and in the process improve his own skills in aerial gunnery. Unlike all other cut-and-dried systems within the RAF, the Bomber Crew selection process was a much more random and informal affair. All the potential crew members of that intake, from pilots to Tail-End-Charlies, were collected together in one of the bigger huts, often with a pint of beer, to help smooth the process, and basically told not to bother to come out of the hut until they had a complete crew around them. As it was a system that had worked incredibly well for years, RAF logic was that there was therefore no need to change it. It was during such a gathering that Victor joined up with his first crew, Forde, Warner, Rollins, Carruthers and Roe.

Once the crew had chosen itself, it was then tasked with getting the hang of working together coherently in their new aircraft. This meant perfecting the individual role of each member of the team and then putting all these functions together. This would then enable them to go where the RAF wanted them to go, and to do what the RAF wanted them to do, which generally speaking from their Lordship's point of view, was to drop some bombs on the enemy, come home, have a rest, then go and do it all again. Over the ten to twelve weeks at Lossiemouth, during the late summer and early autumn of 1943, this team work was what Victor's crew and dozens of others like them spent their time doing. Obviously the main workload at this stage of training fell on the shoulders of the pilot and navigator, with the rest of the crew generally along for the ride. That said, from Victor's point of view, every hour in 'his' turret gave him increased confidence and a feeling of being more at home with his role in proceedings. Occasionally they were allocated the odd target for Victor to have a shot at, but everyone fully understood the need for the new Pilot and Navigator to get the preferential treatment with this phase of training.

Now those few short weeks had passed by, and things were really starting to gel for them as a crew, so they received their posting and were on the way south to RAF Driffield in South Yorkshire to 466 Squadron. 466 Squadron was a bit of an oddity as it was a Royal Australian Air Force (RAAF) medium bomber unit flying Wellingtons made up mainly of English crews. History shows that over time it became more and more Australian populated, but when Victor and his crew arrived, the Queen's English was very much the accent of choice. However, at one and the same time 466 Squadron was getting its Wellingtons replaced by one of the range of four engine bombers now available to the RAF. Their allocation of machinery was the Handley-Page Halifax. Understandably their time on the Wellington was short and only seven sorties were recorded, between Sunday 22 August and the following Tuesday. LN442 and LN443 were the two Wellingtons Victor used, with five mine-laying operations just off on the north German coast near the Friesian Islands and the west coast of France close to Royen.

Victor's time on Wellingtons provided just two bombing operations, though only one sortie was fully completed. The bombsight equipment failed on LN442 during the operation of the 31st which unfortunately resulted in an aborted mission. Thus the Forde crew all logged their first RTB in their personal logbooks. With the conversion to the Halifax it naturally meant that for Victor and the rest of his crew it was off on their travels again for another six weeks' training as they learned to handle to their new rather larger and somewhat heavier plane. It was a full six-week course for the whole Squadron and would be operated by 1652 CU based at RAF Marston Moor. Marston Moor was in South Yorkshire, just some thirty-five to forty miles inland from RAF Driffield, and it was here the Forde crew was joined by Sgts Quirke and Cole to make the full team. Sgt Eyles would join them a little later as second Bomb Aimer, when Bert Warner was trained up to use the new H2S navigation and targeting system,

At this point it may well be worth recalling the various differences between the two planes. Officially the Wellington was designated a medium bomber and the Halifax a heavy. Therefore the former had just two radial engines and the latter four of the fabulous Rolls-Royce V12 Merlins. Both had been derived from earlier unsuccessful twin-engine designs, and in many ways were rather similar until you read the Bomb Load Data Sheet. Here the Halifax won hands down with a load capacity almost three times that of the Wellington. Other than that the Wellington was a little shorter, weighed a little less, and was not quite so large in all other major dimensions. It was some twenty to twenty-five miles an hour slower and had a significantly shorter range of 1,360 against the Halifax's 1,860. Interestingly it had a service ceiling some 4,000 feet higher than the Halifax and as such could climb to and operate at 22,000 feet. Obviously the main factors in the favour of the Halifax were the greater payload and the greater operational range, all to the satisfaction of Bomber Command, but making harder work for Victor and the rest of the crew. Nonetheless it was a great training aircraft for their ultimate goal, the Avro Lancaster, more of which a little later.

Coincidentally the conversion to the Handley-Page Halifax yielded exactly the same amount of operational sorties as the Wellington. This time the seven operations more or less spanned the Christmas and New Year period of 1943-1944. Their first Halifax sortie was on 20 December and the last one on 7 January. On the third sortie, 'The Big City', Berlin was the target, but it was not until the raid following the Berlin run that Victor mentioned anything about enemy action. In that post-raid report it was noted that their plane HX266 had collected some flak damage from what was believed to be radar controlled ack-ack guns in the Wilhelmshaven area. Fortunately according to this report after the raid, it produced only a slight amount of damage to the aircraft and none to the crew. The other high point Victor noted from his time on the Halifax occurred just three days later, landing out at Tangmere, as their Halifax LV837 ran low on fuel and their pilot John Forde made a precautionary diversion into the Kent fighter airfield to take on more.

In all the Halifax raids, they were led to the target area by the Lancasters of the Pathfinder Force, whom they were to join in just a few weeks' time. This way, like many others before them, Victor and the rest of the John Forde team had been given a good insight into what was needed to be a Pathfinder crew, long before they ever started their PFF training. As it turned out, the Halifax posting was a superb learning programme from every aspect. That said, it was in reality just another stepping stone for them all in reaching their ultimate goal and becoming a member of that elite organisation.

4

# Pathfinders

So just six months after stepping into a Bomber for the first time, Victor's latest posting was sending him further south in mainland Britain to RAF Graveley in Huntingdonshire, to join the *crème de la crème* of Bomber Command, the Pathfinder Force (PFF). He was off to RAF Graveley where he would be joining 35 Squadron, one of the earliest and most prestigious of the Pathfinder Force Squadrons. Once he had received the posting and before he even stepped foot past the gate house for the first time, he realised that there had already been many pages of history written by this unique group of very special airmen. He reminded himself that would do well to read up, ask questions and learn as much about his new colleagues as he could.

## The PFF

When Victor Roe joined the RAF, no one could deny that it was in a pretty desperate state. More particularly his part of it, Bomber Command, was in a critical, life-threatening situation. Losses were very high and at an almost unsustainable level, not only that the success rate, at best, was very poor. Something had to be done, and quickly. That something turned out to be the Pathfinders.

The story of Don Bennett's Pathfinder squadrons has been the subject of a number of excellent books over the years. Somehow it seems that every time a new Pathfinder story is unearthed and recounted, new facets of the operations of that elite team are unearthed and yet more acts of heroism of its airmen are unearthed and told. Victor Roe's story is no exception to this well-established pattern.

In the early days of the Second World War, there was no such thing as accurate bombing on either side of the conflict. To make it work, 'Carpet Bombing' techniques similar to the method used by the Luftwaffe for the London Blitz had to be employed. For more specific targets, occasional lucky hits did 'a little' to improve the percentage accuracy figures of the mainstream of the Bomber Command crews of the day; but in all honesty the real description should not have been 'little', but 'very little'. The effect of most bombing raids was minimal. This was identified in August

1941 by the Butt Report, which made very uncomfortable reading for everyone in the RAF above the rank of Sergeant. The RAF's policy of daylight raids with light and medium bombers, with no fighter escort was just plain wrong, and furthermore its equipment was rather basic and nowhere near as reliable as it should have been. It was also made obvious that crew training and practice sorties were all very much shorter than the crews actually required to do their job successfully.

Unsurprisingly the raids at that time failed to achieve any significant results, apart from a nuisance value from a military perspective, and the terrorising of the civilian populations of the general area below. Neither action was in the slightest bit useful in the terms of military progress. The enemy authorities usually only took a short while to shrug off the effects of the odd accurate bombing raid on one of their installations, and somehow the effect on the civilians was usually to create a level of anger against the enemy that further encouraged their resolve to continue supporting their leaders. This was exactly the reaction that the German bombing had promoted during the Blitz on London and other major British cities. The effect of this bombing was obviously not having the desired military or civilian result for either side.

However, whilst the German leadership, especially Adolf Hitler himself, dreamt of all manner of vengeance weapons (latterly becoming the V1, V2 and short-lived V3) and other wonder weapons to win the war, the RAF High Command decided that actually dropping the ordnance they already had available on the enemy's positions, rather than in fields a couple of miles away, might in fact have quicker and more positive results. As such something urgently needed to be done to sharpen up the accuracy of the aircrews at the delivery end of Bomber Command. That was where the Pathfinder Force came in.

Arthur 'Bomber' Harris, Commander in Chief, Bomber Command, later Air Chief Marshal Sir Arthur Harris, GCB, OBE, AFC was the man who chose the Australian, Don Bennett, to form and run the new unit. Bennett had known Harris for several years before this and they had worked together during the heydays of flying boats in the 1930s. Harris knew of Bennett's exceptional skills in navigation first hand and to him this would be the key to achieving the required improvement in bombing accuracy. Bennett was tasked with improving the bombing efficiency and therefore the overall operational effectiveness of the RAF. In essence he had to make every bomb count. Easy enough to say, but a somewhat harder thing to put into practice.

On his appointment on 5 July 1942, Bennett was allocated five bomber squadrons comprising wherever possible of the best crews that could be mustered for the aircraft types available, particularly with reference to the navigation aspects of their work. Needless to say, this poaching of the best crews from other squadrons did not make him, or the Pathfinders, the most popular people around the corridors of RAF High Command. Furthermore, when it was decided that they should also have their own airfields, a number of quite senior RAF officers were more than a little unhappy, and expressed their disapproval. The initial Pathfinder squadron formation was:

- No. 7 Squadron, No. 35 Squadron, No. 83 Squadron, No. 156 Squadron and No. 109 Squadron. They flew a mixed bag of aircraft: Stirlings (7 Sqn), Halifaxes (35 Sqn), Lancasters (83 Sqn) and Wellingtons (156 Sqn and 109 Sqn), although 109 Sqn would very quickly be allocated the new de Havilland Mosquito, as that aircraft became a mainstream part of the Pathfinders inventory.

At about the same time it became blindingly obvious that it was only by bombing at night that the RAF loss rates would be pegged back to a more acceptable level. But with limited resources at his disposal, even the increased accuracy of the PFF methods, and the ability to choose either Mosquitos or Lancasters, or a mixture of both to lead and mark a raid, the decision had to be made for the PFF to aim at the larger targets and pass up the more remote chance of hitting individual pin-point targets. That added sophistication could come a little later. The second part of that theory followed the lines:

> If you hit the town in general, you may get lucky and hit part of the factory, but for sure you will de-house many of the factory's workforce and with a bit of extra luck you get a 'full house' and also play havoc with the local transport infrastructure and knock out a few roads and railway lines as a bonus.

As mentioned to Victor many times before, every bomb needed to count.

The basic operating format of the Pathfinders would be to use high precision navigation to find the target area or town. They would fly ahead of the main bomber force, and then use coloured flares and coloured smoke markers to indicate the exact bombing point to aim at, whether it was a factory, an airfield, or a railway or road junction etc. Using this very practical system, even if the markers missed the exact aiming point, the following bombers had the opportunity to correctly place their ordnance, simply by being told to bomb to the north, south, east or west of the coloured marker. It was a system that improved the accuracy of Bomber Command by a hitherto un-imaginable amount, and slowly but surely enabled them to start eating into the German industrial capacity to produce war materials.

Needless to say, these Pathfinder planes also carried a good cross section of the normal ordnance available to RAF Bomber Command. Thus all Pathfinder bomb aimers were quite comfortable to include several thousands of pounds of high explosive or incendiary bombs amongst the munitions they delivered on any given raid. After all, a few glowing fires in the target area as well as the flares dropped earlier, could only assist the main bomber stream, due to arrive on site a few minutes behind them.

Obviously, with its 'friends in high places', and the pressing needs of the war, which at that stage was obviously not going at all well, the Pathfinders also had access to the most modern and sophisticated planes and the latest navigational equipment available. This included the latest versions of the new wonder invention, radar. The best crews were also on the Pathfinder 'must have' list, particularly, those with the most experience, the best grasp of the latest technology and those capable of achieving a high standard of training. They were ferreted out and all brought into the fold of this select group, all to improve the bombing accuracy, and the strategic benefits it would produce.

Because of this in December 1942 the Oboe Navigation Project was brought into the fold, to add to Gee and H2S as the most sophisticated and accurate of the latest electronic navigation and bombing systems available to the new group.


## H2S

H2S was basically a ground mapping radar carried on board the aircraft, the scanner being housed in a large bulge underneath the aircraft, to the rear of the bomb bay. H2S radar had one major disadvantage, in that the enemy learned to identify the radar transmissions and night fighters could then be directed towards the aircraft.


## Oboe

Oboe was a form of distance measuring equipment, virtually immune from interference and rated as the most precise bombing aid of the war. Its weakness was that, in the early days, it could only be used by one aircraft at a time. Because of this the Pathfinder leaders became the main early users of Oboe. Later versions could handle fifty aircraft at a time.


## Gee

Gee was similar to Oboe, using signal transmission times to calculate aircraft position. It had a great advantage that it could handle a larger number of aircraft at any one time, but was somewhat less accurate than Oboe.

The formation, in September 1942, of the first of the Pathfinder squadrons was the fledgling beginnings of an organisation in which Victor was to become an integral part. As decreed, only the best were recruited, and despite some pretty strong protestations from various squadron, wing, and station commanders, who were understandably very loathe to lose their most experienced pilots and crews, the orders to the Pathfinder Force's CO left no one in any doubt as to the new organisation's place in the wider scheme of things. They had priority and they were to start their work the same day that they became operational; there was simply no time to lose.

The initial airfields chosen by Bennett were Wyton and Oakington, with Warboys and Gravely as their satellites. The allocation of the first squadrons would be 35

Squadron to Gravely, 7 Squadron to Oakington, 83 Squadron to Wyton, and 156 Squadron to Warboys. Designated No. 3 Group, Castle Hill House in Huntingdon would later become the Administration Centre for the whole of the Pathfinder operation.

On the night of 18–19 August 1942 the Pathfinders (now also designated the PFF for official purposes) made their first attack on the enemy, on the north German town of Flensburg near the Danish border. Due to exceptionally bad weather and an unreported shift in wind direction it was a total failure. In fact more bombs landed in Denmark than in Germany. Flensburg itself was stated to have been completely untouched by the bombers. They would have to do better ... much better. Unfortunately the second mission, to Frankfurt on 23–24 August shared the same fate. It too was a complete and total failure. They did get closer to the enemy this time, but also closer to the very active enemy defences. The PFF lost five aircraft for very little gain, not quite the start Don Bennett had hoped for.

However two days later, Kassel was the unfortunate German town that was at the receiving end when the PFF got it right for the first time. Many buildings were flattened, including several in use by the German military. Also demolished was a reasonable percentage of the Henschel aircraft engine factory. The Pathfinder Force was really up and running.

The next three raids to Saarbrücken, Saarlouis and Karlsruhe met with mixed success as the PFF system was further fine-tuned. The consensus was that while the Pathfinders got to target on time, the following main bomber streams did not, so when they arrived it was not unusual for most of the markers to have burned out. This meant that they had no option but to bomb on the few markers that were left burning. As such the following planes bombed on the final TIs to fall, which frequently marked just the furthest edges of the target and were an outer limit only. Thus the main weight of bombs started on the edge of target, or worse still, off-target and continued to spread back along the line of the attacking aircraft, away from the intended area. The process was given the name 'creep-back' and it needed to be eliminated.

Once they had the data to hand, the planners of the Pathfinder-led raids then had the chance to revise their methods of dropping marker flares and backing them up to counter this.

In order to counteract creep-back, the Pathfinder force on each raid was split into three groups. One group, the Illuminators, dropped navigational flares marking the route to the target. The second group, the Visual Markers, would accurately drop target indicators, relatively short burning coloured flares. Then the third group, the Backers-Up, would drop their loads on the flares of the visual markers. The backers up would carry 4,000-lb cookies and a large load of incendiary bombs which would start much more intensive and long lasting fires in the target area. The Main Force bombers would then be able to locate the conflagration from a considerable distance and once over the target could drop their bombs into the fires below.

This would then enable the Master Bomber on the day to produce the regular and constant marking pattern needed be able to achieve the accuracy they were all looking for. This revised system was used for the first time on the Bremen raid, overnight on 4-5 September. On this occasion it was a total success and the revised system brought about the destruction of over 9,000 houses which in effect demolished the homes of almost the entire workforce of the Weserflug aircraft plant. It also inflicted major damage on the Atlas Shipyard just six miles to the south as well as most of the associated warehousing complex. The new system had obviously solved the problem.

By 9–10 September they had this method of operating firmly in place and during the raid on Düsseldorf they managed again to destroy over fifty individual factory buildings as well as many thousands of houses, bombing some 20,000 war workers out of their homes and in many cases out of their jobs. This was the sort of success they were hoping to see. However, the reason behind this success was easy enough to figure out and the German defence controllers had soon worked out what was happening. This first wave of RAF planes was used to hit the targets and leave smoking fires and coloured flares for the second wave that carried the main force of the raid. It therefore was obvious that the first wave of bombers were the ones they had to try to knock out of the sky or divert before they could even get the raid under way. It was also surmised that a proliferation of false flares and fires, hastily lit a couple of miles away from areas being attacked, could well be distracting to incoming planes so they would maybe be tricked into hitting the open countryside instead. Many brains were put to work in Germany to find ways to curb this new effective method employed by RAF Bomber Command.

One very successful PFF innovation was the introduction of a Master Bomber whose duty it was to first mark the target and then to remain over the target, above the main PFF markers, directing their efforts. This would enable the Master Bomber on the day to produce the regular and constant marking pattern needed be able to achieve the accuracy they were all looking for. He could also advise the Main Force if any false flares and fires were ignited by the enemy. The first raid with a Master Bomber was on the night of 20 June 1943 against the Zeppelin works in Friedrichshafen.

By late December, Don Bennett had managed to acquire some of the bomber variant of the new de Havilland 'wonder plane' the Mosquito, and by the night of 20-21 December they were put into service. Not that this would be of any interest to Victor, as these small sleek, ultra-fast machines were a two-man crew; a pilot and a navigator/bomb aimer. It was so fast and could outrun anything flying at the time by quite some margin, that it was deemed un-necessary to weigh it down with any guns at all. With the pilot merely firewalling the throttle if in any danger, the plane inevitably was out of enemy range within seconds. The more traditional Lancaster would therefore remain the platform for Victor's workstation.

By 1943, the Stirling, the first of the RAF's four-engine heavy bombers was phased out of the PFF inventory and the Lancaster became the prime workhorse for the Pathfinders as the supply of Mosquitos built up to meet the demand. By this time there was but a single Halifax squadron left operational in the Pathfinder Force, as it was phased out and replaced. Unsurprisingly, the following year that too had been phased out of the PFF and Bennett's squadrons were made up entirely of Lancasters and Mosquitos, with the de Havilland aircraft becoming superior in squadron numbers, by war's end.

With this increase in size of the Pathfinder operation, Bennett and his men obviously needed more airfields to operate from. As a Lancaster man, this impinged little on Victor's life, as the greater majority of this growth was to accommodate the arrival of more Mosquito Squadrons and thus Bourne, Granston Lodge, Upwood, Downham Market and Little Staughton were added to the PFF's real estate. 1409 (Met) Flight was an essential part of the PFF, supplying met and navigational data to both the RAF and the USAAF. It was allocated a home at Wyton, where it stayed for the remainder of the war while the Lancaster PFF Training Flight settled in just a mile or two down the road from RAF Wyton, at RAF Warboys. Wyton and Warboys were so close in fact, that the circuits used by the squadrons' aircraft, marked out on the ground by the 'Drem' lights actually overlapped!

The success they were now enjoying enabled some added scope to their tactics and use within Bomber Command. Now it made sense to let a few Pathfinder planes lead smaller raids to attack less obvious key targets, as well as 'saving' them for the big monster raids that were starting to become rather popular with the politicians and war leaders. As you can imagine, the pace of the bomber offensive was really starting to pick up and at least one squadron of Pathfinders were in action virtually every night, leading and marking a raid somewhere over Europe. All this of course was added to by desire of the UK's leadership to attack the German capital, Berlin, every twenty-four hours. This way the BBC could announce on the news, every morning, 'Aircraft from Bomber Command attacked Berlin again last night'. It was believed to be a morale-boosting announcement that was of major importance to the civilian population.

The Essen raid on 20–21 June was the one that eventually convince any lingering doubters that the PFF could deliver what it had promised. Fifty-three buildings in the giant Krupp factory complex in the centre of town were pretty much destroyed, along with 160 acres of roads, sidings, storage yards and other war essential infrastructure. The target also had the added bonus of being situated between two main railway lines, so any stray bombs undershooting or overshooting the target were almost certain to have landed in or on the railways system.

By the end of the year it was estimated that the bulk of any RAF bomber stream was putting its ordnance within a three-mile radius of the PFF Target Indicators, quite a significant step up from the previous year's scores of 'Zero on Target'. These results were more to the politicians liking, and reflected well on Bomber Command.

The Pathfinder Force had grown steadily throughout its existence.

1942  4 Squadrons
1943  10 Squadrons
1944  19 Squadrons
1945  21 Squadrons

To put this into perspective, by the end of hostilities, it was estimated that the PFF had something in the order of 300 to 350 aircraft and approximately 14,000 to 15,000 personnel. Although on a day-to-day basis, these figures were always a somewhat movable feast and the war's end did nothing to change matters, except the knowledge that virtually all personnel changes now were postings rather than MIA or KIA. Furthermore, due to the exceptional survival rate of the Mosquito, the PFF had an impressively good loss rate overall, especially when one considers what they were being asked to do. However as the Mosquito's loss rate was superbly low, running at an enviable 0.7 per cent, it did of course mean the Lancasters were almost as vulnerable in the PFF as they were in the main bomber stream, with the exception of the small element of surprise they might have gained by being first over the target.

It may be interesting at this point to note Don Bennett's recorded thoughts at the time on the comparisons between the two main aircraft types available to him, the Mosquito and the Lancaster. The Bennett conundrum goes something like this.

If the Mosquito is equal to several Lancasters, but a Mosquito carries half the bomb load of a Lancaster on a Berlin raid, its casualty rate is about one tenth of the Lancaster, its cost is one third that of the Lancaster and it has a crew of two instead of seven . . . discuss.

It is, as you can see, the sort of mathematical puzzle that is doomed never to produce an answer convincing to everyone. In hindsight, it was just very fortunate that Don Bennett had both aircraft types available to him when he needed them most, and of course the crews made up of airmen like Victor to fly in them.

As the war drew to a close, and a euphoric peace descended across a battered Europe, the Mosquitos carried on with their weather forecasting role, and the Lancasters were put to good use taking food to the starving Dutch population, ferrying home Prisoners of War just as quickly as they could and of course providing the continuation of training sorties to keep the crews sharp. Other Mosquitos were earmarked for a diplomatic postal service through the Allied sections of occupied Europe and a number of Lancasters started to head abroad for operations elsewhere, or were sold to other countries. Sadly it was at this stage that many others were lined up ready for scrapping, selling or for spares, on dispersal areas of countless airfields nationwide that were now rapidly becoming non-operational.

The Pathfinders flew their last full operational mission on Wednesday 3 May 1945, having completed a staggering 50,490 sorties. In some three short years of operation they had attacked 3,440 separate targets which by simple maths alone equates to three or four targets per night, every night from their formation until the end of the war. In the process they had lost 3,318 brave young men, with many more injured. Of the survivors several thousand more had been shot down and forced to spend the final part of the conflict as uninvited guests of the Germans, in POW camps scattered throughout the European mainland. Many of the captured PFF crews in that situation made it home, but many others did not.

The Pathfinders had done a magnificent job, of that no one was in any doubt. Don Bennett's thoughts on the matter are recorded in Chapter Eleven. Sadly Victor was to be one of their last casualties.

## Pathfinder Order of Battle

### September 1942

| | | |
|---|---|---|
| Graveley | 35 Squadron | Halifax |
| Oakington | 7 Squadron | Stirling |
| Wyton | 83 Squadron | Lancaster |
| Warboys | 156 Squadron | Wellington |

| | | |
|---|---|---|
| December 1943 | Headquarters, No. 8 Group. Huntingdon | |

| | | |
|---|---|---|
| Graveley | 35 Squadron | Halifax |
| Oakington | 7 Squadron | Lancaster |
| | 627 Squadron | Mosquito |
| Wyton | 83 Squadron | Lancaster |
| | 139 Squadron | Mosquito |
| Bourn | 97 Squadron | Lancaster |
| Warboys | 156 Squadron | Lancaster |
| Gransden Lodge | 405 (RACF) Squadron | Lancaster |
| Marham | 105 Squadron | Mosquito |
| | 109 Squadron | Mosquito |

| | | |
|---|---|---|
| December 1944 | Headquarters, No. 8 Group. Huntingdon | |

| | | |
|---|---|---|
| Graveley | 35 Squadron | Lancaster |
| | 83 Squadron | Lancaster |
| | 97 Squadron | Lancaster |
| | 692 Squadron | Mosquito |
| Oakington | 7 Squadron | Lancaster |
| | 571 Squadron | Mosquito |
| Wyton | 128 Squadron | Mosquito |
| | 1409 Squadron (Met Flight) | Mosquito |

| Bourne | 105 Squadron | Mosquito |
|---|---|---|
| | 162 Squadron | Mosquito |
| Gransden Lodge | 142 Squadron | Mosquito |
| | 405 (RACF) Squadron | Lancaster |
| Upwood | 156 Squadron | Lancaster |
| | 139 Squadron | Mosquito |
| Downham Market | 635 Squadron | Lancaster |
| | 608 Squadron | Mosquito |
| Little Staughton | 582 Squadron | Lancaster |
| | 109 Squadron | Mosquito |
| Warboys | PFF Training Unit | Lancaster |

March 1945,        Headquarters, No. 8 Group. Huntingdon

| Graveley | 35 Squadron | Lancaster |
|---|---|---|
| | 83 Squadron | Lancaster (Detached to No. 5 Group) |
| | 97 Squadron | Lancaster |
| | 692 Squadron | Mosquito |
| Wyton | 128 Squadron | Mosquito |
| | 163 Squadron | Mosquito |
| | 1409 Squadron (Met Flight) | Mosquito |
| Oakington | 7 Squadron | Lancaster |
| | 627 Squadron | Mosquito |
| Bourne | 105 Squadron | Mosquito |
| | 162 Squadron | Mosquito |
| Gransden Lodge | 142 Squadron | Mosquito |
| | 405 (RACF) Squadron | Lancaster |
| Upwood | 156 Squadron | Lancaster |
| | 139 Squadron | Mosquito |
| Downham Market | 635 Squadron | Lancaster |
| | 608 Squadron | Mosquito |
| | 627 Squadron | Mosquito (Detached to No. 5 Group) |
| Little Staughton | 582 Squadron | Lancaster |
| | 109 Squadron | Mosquito |
| Warboys | PFF Training Unit | Lancaster |

## Nomenclature of Individual Pathfinder Operational Functions

At this stage it may well be appropriate to briefly outline the various roles allotted by the Pathfinder System and the PFF names by they were known. It was this comprehensive interlocking of each set of aircraft roles devised by Bennett and his team that made the Pathfinders so successful.

### Master Bomber

Over all, literally, was the Master Bomber, whose role was to direct the entire operation from a position high above the target zone. In theory they were the first into the target zone and the last to leave. This was always a risky place to be, made more worrying for the top brass back in England, as it was a job that could only be carried out by someone with a vast amount of experience, i.e. an officer and an experienced crew they could ill afford to lose.

### Deputy Master Bomber

No. 2 in lead group and back up to Master Bomber.

### Windower

Although taken over in the later stages of the war by the Mosquitoes of the LNSF (Light Night Striking Force), the dropping of the tinfoil 'Window' clouds to confuse the German radar was originally all part and parcel of the mainstream Pathfinder Force operation.

### Route Marker

As the name implies these planes primary role was to drop long lasting marker flares at the turning points on the routes in to the target. The Route Marker Flares, were also designated Land Markers when dropped within fifteen or twenty miles of the target area.

### Sky Marker

These Pathfinder planes were the ones allocated the dropping of parachute flares when the undercast was impenetrable and conventional TIs would either disappear through the cloud or glare in such a way as to make them unusable.

### Blind Marker

Pathfinder planes designated to drop marker flares through cloud cover when it was believed they could work normally and provide guidance.

### Blind Backer-up

Pathfinder planes that were located in the main bomber stream, to renew the flares of the Blind Markers as they started to burn out.

*Visual Marker*
A Pathfinder plane whose job was to operate at a much lower altitude than the rest
the of the attacking force and pinpoint mark the very centre of the target area with
TIs.

*Visual Marker Backer-up*
Usually a job allocated to an inexperienced crew, to give them the opportunity to get
some 'on the job' training.

*Supporter*
This was the usually the first job for any new Pathfinder Crew. They were asked
to follow the primary markers in to the target zones, ahead of the main bomber
stream and make it difficult for the defenders to work out which was the Master
Bomber and also to drop the first 'bombs only' load in as accurately as possible to
the markers and hopefully set the pattern for the rest of the raid.

*Primary Visual Marker*
These boys were the experienced crews who were to supplement or replace the
Visual Markers. Really they were the main target markers for the following bombers
in the main bomber stream.

*Long Stop*
Obviously things did not always go to plan and sometimes there needed to be a
system of 'cancelling' an incorrect marker, by placing a different colour flare next to
it. That was the job of the Long Stop.

*Backer-up*
It was common practice for most designated Pathfinder roles to have at least one
plane behind it in the stream, ready and able to take over should the primary plane
encounter technical problems, get shot down or taken out by flak.

*Main Bomber Stream*
The non-Pathfinder Force bombers from Bomber Command who followed the
PFF markers in to the attack and generally made up the bulk of the aircraft of any
bomber operation on enemy positions.


## RAF Graveley and 35 Squadron

RAF Graveley was situated just to the north east of the market town of St Neots
in Cambridgeshire, close to the Huntingdonshire–Cambridgeshire border. It was
located on the opposite (eastern) side of the A1 trunk road just two miles further

to the north than the town itself. It was one of the four initial airfields, selected by Don Bennett for his new force, all of which were within reasonable reach of the town of Huntingdon; useful, as by 1943 Huntingdon would be Bennett's choice of headquarters for 8 Group for the remainder of the war. RAF Graveley was also home to 83, 97, 622 and of course 35 Squadron, Victor's operational squadron during his time as a Pathfinder Force rear gunner.

RAF Graveley had a number of claims to fame. It was the first operational RAF station to be equipped with the experimental Fog Investigation Dispersal Operation system (FIDO). It was also the bomber station where the first H2S airborne radar systems were put to squadron use and it was Victor's squadron, 35 Squadron, which was selected along with 7 Squadron, to fit and operate this new device. H2S was on the whole, a pretty good system, but it was by no means perfect.

RAF Graveley was built during the big airfield push in 1941–42 along with several others in the local area. It was a standard A Class airfield with three intersecting concrete runways. The main east–west runway was 2,000 yards, (headings 120 × 300) and the two cross runways 1,400 yards, (headings 190 × 010) and (headings 230 × 050). All had the standard 50 yards width. It had hard standings for thirty-six heavy aircraft outside and three standard RAF hangers for more serious maintenance and repair work, two of the T2 design and one of the B1s. It had facilities for some 3,000 personnel of all ranks including WAAFs, and the full team comprising of aircrew, ground crew, administrators and all the support trades needed to run a large, diverse yet efficient operation.

When the Pathfinders took it over on 15 August 1942, Graveley had been in use since 1 March that year by the mixed fleet of 616 (Special Duty) Squadron, who spent the war dropping special agents all over Europe on behalf of the Government's shadowy group, the Special Operations Executive (SOE). After 616 moved on, their mongrel fleet was followed by the medium bombers of 26 OTU. It then played a part in the launch of some Vickers Wellingtons on some of the first '1,000 bomber' raids that Bomber Command had started to employ as the RAF gathered strength. It was however the Handley-Page Halifaxes of 35 Squadron that would be the initial Pathfinder unit in place, and the first to start leading Bomber Command on their regular nightly runs out over mainland Europe. The Halifaxes would remain 35 Squadron's primary heavy bomber until the newer Avro Lancaster was phased in.

FIDO, the fog dispersal system was installed along Graveley's main east–west runway early in 1943, and it was no lesser personage than AOC 8 Group, Don Bennett himself who flew the acceptance tests on Thursday 18 February. FIDO was a system that could temporarily clear a runway of fog by lifting the dense foggy air off the tarmac. It did this by firing updrafts of heated air powered by jets of burning petrol along the runway edges, thus partially drying and lifting the damp, heavy air over the runway. This allowed the returning bombers to complete a safe, if somewhat 'hairy' landing. The system could only produce a temporary window of clearance, but usually one that was more than good enough. Bennett was quick to spot its potential and soon became an ardent supporter of the system. It proved to be another of his inspired decisions. However it had to wait many months until much later that same year before weather conditions at Graveley were again poor enough that it could be tested under real fog conditions. In the autumn of 1943 it was used on a particularly foggy occasion to assist four Handley-Page Halifaxes to land in just 100-yard visibility. Needless to say it soon went on to be installed on fourteen other RAF airfields and without doubt saved hundreds of allied aircrew lives during the course of the war. It also helped keep the PFF and Bomber Command fully operational during some of the poorest weather conditions, probably at a time when the German military suspected they would be granted a short reprieve due to their forecasts for the English weather.

On Saturday 1 January 1944, the first of the Mosquitos of 692 Squadron arrived and five weeks later by 1 February they had started to participate in the Pathfinder duties with their larger and heavier cousins. Later that month, modifications to the Mosquitos' bomb carrying and delivery system allowed them to really 'up' their payload and start to carry the larger 4,000-lb 'cookie' bomb. About that same time, the recently formed 571 Squadron arrived at Graveley with their Mosquitos from Downham Market, in Norfolk. They spent a short period attached to 692 Squadron, undergoing the specialised PFF training for LNSF duties and flying the combat sorties and training operations with 692 Squadron and generally learning the ropes. The crews from 571 Squadron then headed off the few miles along the road to set up in business for themselves at RAF Oakington, some ten miles due west of Graveley.

The last combat sortie flown by 35 Squadron out of RAF Graveley was on 25 April 1945, when eight of 35 Squadron's Lancasters were called upon to mark and attack the battery of gun emplacements on one of the Friesian Islands, Wangerooge, just four miles off the north German coast. It was just seven weeks and three days after Victor had been killed. Operationally 35 Squadron and RAF Graveley then fell silent.

A very short time after the conflict was officially over, statisticians, historians and pundits soon got to work collating, analysing, researching, and coordinating the myriad of RAF and Bomber Command numbers. It became obvious that even when you took into account it being one of RAF Graveley's oldest and longest serving squadrons, 35 Squadron, had been an exceptional unit. It had supplied the PFF with hundreds of top quality airmen whose individual tally of completed combat operations often numbered around the hundred sorties each, with some even greater. It was a truly outstanding performance, one that any RAF Station would be quite rightly proud of.

# 5

# Operations—April–June 1944

The passing of time, Victor's untimely demise and the inevitable cross-over between training flights, training operations and full blown squadron raids has pushed Victor's early operational flight record into a slightly grey area that officially leaves us with just an orderly list of the bare facts. Fortunately access to the logbooks of other members of the John Forde crew, particularly Sgts Cole and Caruthers, has added important depth and substance to some of the more clinical aspects of the various squadron reports. The key players in this first part of Victor's RAF career were W/O John (Jack) Forde, Pilot—W/O John (Rolly) Rollins, Navigator—W/O H. (Bert) Warner, Bomb Aimer—Sgt Don Carruthers, Mid Upper Gunner—Sgt A. Smith, Radio Operator—Sgt Doug Cole, Flight Engineer —Sgt Victor (Vic) Roe, Rear Gunner. This was to be the core team for many, many months and a rather well polished and profession team it turned out to be.

Also in a similar grey area for supporting documentation is Victor's private and family life. Despite the fragmenting effect of his family's early history, or maybe because of it, it was more or less about this time that Victor started to feel the need to trace as many of his siblings as he could. We do know he already had some form of contact with his elder sister Kate, as she was listed as next of kin in his RAF records. Kate still lived in Norwich and would soon be married to Ernest Foyster. His older brothers Wilfred and Bertie had both been Fegan's boys, so perhaps that was a sensible starting point for his searches, or maybe Kate had been able to shed some light on their whereabouts. What is known is that he and Wilfred were in fact both now in the military and when Victor got to his permanent posting at 35 Squadron, at RAF Graveley; they were in fact stationed within a few miles of each other. So once they had met up, Victor was able to maintain the contact he was keen to have. This included both of them managing to obtain leave at the same time so that they could occasionally meet up and spend time together back in Norfolk.

## Vickers Wellington

Victor's first ever full squadron combat sortie was with 466 Squadron out of Leconfield on Saturday 22 August 1943. He and his crew were allocated mine laying duties in Vickers Wellington LN443, squadron code HD-T. They had already flown eighteen separate training sorties on Wellingtons prior to this. The training included both day and night cross-country exercises, fighter affiliation exercises, bombing and gunnery practice and a couple of the mandatory pre-operational aircraft test flights. In all they had amassed some twelve hours and thirty-six minutes on type with 466 Squadron, prior to the first combat operation. Not a vast amount and barely a quarter of the time allocated today for a civilian type conversion, but considered enough by the training standards of the day.

In the following week they swapped between that plane and its sister ship LN442 continuing the mine laying process all along the channel coastline, just off the German and French beaches. They were all night sorties and were conducted on the 22, 23 and 24 August. They then moved to the forward base of Stanton Harcourt, a satellite airfield of Abingdon OTU in Oxfordshire, for the raid on Lorient then onward to St Eval on the north coast of Cornwall to prepare for the mine laying operation off the coast of La Rochelle on 27 August. There it appears they encountered their first real experience of enemy searchlights and flak, but recorded no damage during the operation. They returned directly to Stanton Harcourt after the raid. Then for their last two Wellington operations they were asked to try their hand at bombing. The first raid went well, but the bomb aiming equipment failure on their second bombing operation on the 31 August gave them their first Return to Base (RTB) after being in the air for just one hour and twenty minutes. It was their last scheduled trip on the Wellington and heralded their move into the heavy league onto the larger, four-engined Halifax. They were moving up.

## Handley-Page Halifax

As it turned out, their tour of the Halifax was also very short-lived posting. It started with a three-week conversion course at 1652 Conversion Unit that comprised of a further sixteen training sorties, most of which were naturally aimed at John Forde, to give him experience in handling a much heavier aircraft. After being passed as fully operational, they had just seven more operational sorties on the Halifax before moving on, but on this stage of their career Victor and his team had the use of five different Halifax aircraft. Surprisingly, as with their Wellington experience, the last sortie with the Halifax was also an RTB. This short series of raids were spread over two weeks following three week training period at 1652 Conversion Unit.

As expected, the greater majority of the time was allocated to the pilot practising take offs and landings (circuits and bumps in mess parlance), some fifteen hours plus in daylight, then almost seven at night. However the exception to the rule was the exercise on 3 November which was allocated mainly to the gunners with specific practice sessions either side of lunch, one being air to sea and the second air to air. The usual weather tests and fighter affiliation sorties also featured in this build up to full operational status which became effective from Monday 20 December with a bombing raid on Frankfurt. The last operation that Victor had with the Halifax was the raid on Le Mans on Tuesday 7 March 1944. However the most memorable sortie for the whole crew was perhaps the raid on 20 January when they undertook the first of their long trips to Berlin.

Other memorable moments for Victor during this posting involved some slight flak damage over Wilhelmshaven on the operation of 21 February and a precautionary landing at the fighter base at Tangmere in West Sussex just three days later on the 24 February when fuel was running short. They had an overnight stop at Tangmere and headed home the following morning. The Halifax period, however short, did include the crew's introduction to the Pathfinder Marking System and the use of the Coloured Fares, Sky Markers and TIs to get their bombing accuracy right on target. Needless to say that was of course all progressing towards Victor's ultimate goal, a Lancaster in the Pathfinder Force. All this just a few short weeks or so after his first ever Halifax operation. Obviously the plan was slotting neatly into place.

Victor's first Lancaster operation with the PFF was flown with 35 Squadron out of RAF Graveley on Wednesday 26 April 1943, but before that was a further short period of type familiarisation. Over the Easter period, he and his crew had been undergoing the standard PFF Night Training with 35 Squadron's own Navigation Training Unit (NTU) based at the RAF Warboys. They completed ten further training exercises on the Lancaster as they got used to their new kit. It had been a pleasant change for the Forde crew to train 'at home' just up the road at Warboys. For once they did not have to traipse all over the country to yet another far off station in the middle of nowhere, to get converted on to type and then be hauled back to Squadron before they could get started on their real job. With just ten miles between airfields, it meant they would be training over their own piece of countryside. This PFF in-house training unit was another of Don Bennett's good ideas which was most successful and appreciated by all.

## Essen 26-27 April 1944

Lancaster ND731A-Able was the plane allocated to Victor's crew for their first PFF sortie. Although other planes appeared and reappeared in Victor's logbook time and time again, this was his one and only trip in 731. (Later lost on 5 July 1944. Shot down over Villeneuve St Georges). The Railway Marshalling Yards for the city of Essen in the heart of the Ruhr Valley were the targets chosen by High Command to be Victor's first operational sortie as a Pathfinder. His usual pilot F/O John Forde was at the controls as they followed the other Lancasters in the 35 Squadron contingent across the channel towards Germany. There were a total of 492 bombers making the trip that night. The weather forecast for their first operation was for clear skies with mild industrial haze over the target. They were warned they would be leaving conspicuous contrails from their four Rolls-Royce Merlin's exhausts. Not something to dwell on just prior to take off.

The crew of ND731 were as follows:

| | |
|---|---|
| F/O John (Jack) Forde | Pilot |
| F/O H. W. (Bert) Warner | Bomb Aimer |
| W/O John (Rolly) H. Rollins | Navigator |
| Sgt Donald (Don) Carruthers | Radio Operator |
| Sgt William (Bill) Quirke (RAAF) | Mid-Upper Gunner |
| Sgt Victor (Vic) A. Roe | Rear Gunner |
| Sgt Douglas (Doug) A. Cole | Flight Engineer |

Bert Warner, the Bomb Aimer, later became the designated H2S Operator when this new navigation system was introduced to the PFF repertoire. The Germans, by then, had devised ways of locking on to and tracking the H2S signals and so this equipment was used rather sparingly. From then on it was usual for a second Bomb Aimer, Sgt Eyles, to be added to the crew. He then flew as a regular part of the Forde crew.

The ground controllers noted ND731 lift-off time at seven minutes past eleven (23.07 hrs in RAF speak) some seven minutes after the first plane in the bomber stream had taken off and then noted its return time as five minutes to four the next morning (03.55 hrs). Not far short of a five-hour round trip. They had returned to base some fifty minutes after the first of the returning Lancasters from 35 Squadron, the extra time probably being due to the crew's inexperience, as there were no recorded problems with the aircraft.

The official squadron report for ND731 gave no indication of either heavy flak or fighter interception, although flak was observed both in the target area and en route to Essen. One or two aircraft in the bomber stream were hit and at least one from another Pathfinder Squadron had to turn back with flak damage. From the reports we have available, we can assume that Victor's first sortie was relatively gentle and more or less flak and fighter free. Only the facts that they were coned and blinded by searchlights on one occasion and that the marking appeared good, was entered on the crew's additional notes.

At debriefing, the Intelligence Officer also noted that they thought their bomb pattern appeared to be spot on target. These comments were later verified by de-briefing reports from the other PFF squadrons that took part in the same raid. No doubt with the first sortie over, Victor, like the rest of the Forde crew breathed a huge sigh of relief and slept soundly for the first time in ages. Their bomb load for the Essen raid had been one 4,000-lb Minol bomb, three × 500-lb GP (General Purpose) bombs and six × 1,000-lb Medium Capacity bombs. This was a super-heavy load that only the Lancaster was capable of carrying.

## Achères 30 April–1 May 1944

Three days later on Sunday 30 April, Lancaster ND762E-Easy was allocated to the Forde crew for their second trip with 35 Squadron against the enemy. Railway marshalling yards were again the target of choice, but this time they were French, at Achères, just fourteen miles north west of Paris. As with their first trip earlier that week, the weather over the target was fine and clear. All the target indicators were clearly visible and the crew of ND762 were easily able to follow the Master Bomber's instructions and drop their twelve 1,000-lb GP High Explosive ordnance, accurately into the target area. Their radio operator, Sergeant Smith was replaced by the permanent Forde crew member W/O Quirke, other than that, it was the same crew.

The fact that there were three days between the raids did not mean that Victor and his crew had time off or the chance for a lie in or prolonged tea breaks in the mess. These non-combat days were fully utilised by all crews, especially the new boys, to gain practice in night flying, navigating, and target spotting along with perfecting the myriad of skills they needed to make every trip over enemy territory really count. For those crews not on that day's Order of Battle, there were also the flight tests to undertake on each aircraft that was down to take part in that night's sortie, as well as flight tests on aircraft that had undergone major repairs, changes of engines and other non-routine servicing. Victor's crew were allocated training flights on both the 2 and 3 May prior to the Montdidier raid.

## Montdidier 3–4 May 1944

Although they had already been tasked with a training sortie on 3 May, the Forde crew were on the Battle Order for the raid the same night. Their target was the Luftwaffe airfield at Montdidier in Picardy, about sixty miles north of Paris. Again they were assigned ND762 with the call sign E-Easy.

After the usual briefings and segregations they took off at 22.43 in the middle of a tight stream comprising of Lancasters ND703, ND928, Victor's crew in ND762 and ND692; all four getting airborne in four minutes flat. Because of this sort of situation, all rear gunners were tasked with turning their turrets away from the dead astern position during take-off, to avoid any 'unfortunate' accidents. They flew that operation as part of the main force with no specific PFF assignment.

They arrived over target in clear skies on schedule at 00.10, but just as they were starting their run in to target the Master Bomber requested a 'go round' while he re-marked the target area. On the second run in, the Forde crew arrived at much the same time as ND928 with the Hausvick crew on board and at 00.22 both Lancasters ran in together at 10,000 feet and bombed simultaneously. The reported accuracy in the squadron records of their bombing was, 'bang on' and the combined efforts of 726 and 928 were 'concentrated on target'. Not a lot of fun for those on the receiving end, but that was not what Victor was thinking of at that moment, nor the fact that it was just the sort of result that the RAF High Command wanted to hear.

Several of the bombers following Victor's noted that after 726 and 928 had made their attack there was an abnormally large 'white' explosion in the centre of the target area where presumably they had hit something rather special. There was no report of fighters of flak, and they touched down on the Graveley tarmac at 02.40 recording a flight time just a few minutes' short of four hours. Unfortunately Lancaster ND643 which had taken off just ten minutes after Victor's plane was not heard from again and was posted as missing. By a strange twist of fate, the squadron letters on ND643, T-LS, were the same letters that would be on the plane that Victor would be aboard on his last flight, some eleven months later. He was starting to be touched by the effects of war.

Further training flights were allocated on the 5, 6, 7 and 8 May, which surprisingly added some reality to their situation when they were forced to return to the airfield with severe icing on the 5 May and forced to sit out the task on 6 May altogether as the aircraft became unserviceable prior to take off.

## Nantes 6–7 May 1944

E-Easy's next operation was just a few days later on Saturday 6 May, when Victor and the regular Forde crew were designated as a PFF supporter aircraft. They were off to pay a visit the marshalling yards at Nantes, on the River Loire; just over thirty miles inland from the French Atlantic coast. Again they had a good run out and clear skies over target, which was conveniently placed adjacent to the wide silver ribbon that denoted the path of the river. It had been nearly 01.00 when they got airborne, and in a little less than an hour and a half they were on schedule over target, dropping their bomb load at a recorded time of 02.16. It appears from the records that the trip home was equally as uneventful as the run out and they touched down at Graveley at 03.56. For the second time running the planes arriving later in the main bomber stream noted in their reports that they had seen extra-large explosions in the target area shortly after ND762's bomb load had been dropped. This time the accompanying balls of flame were recorded as yellow, so it would be safe to assume that Victor's team had scored a direct hit on a fully loaded wagon or two, whilst in the process of wreaking the expected havoc amongst the jungle of steel rails and points in the yards.

## Haine-St-Pierre 8–9 May 1944

The Forde crew then decamped to ND929J-Jug for the first of several European trips with it spread over the next few weeks. The target for the operation on the night of 8–9 May was more marshalling yards and locomotive sheds this time a little further afield than earlier attacks. It was at Haine-St-Pierre near Charleroi in Belgium and it was to be quite an eventful trip.

Yet again, the weather remained fine and clear, and good results were expected. Victor and his team had a good run out to target and had identified it from quite some distance. 35 Squadron had been preceded by eight PFF Mosquitos also from RAF Graveley, dispensing Window as well as their own 4,000-lb bomb load so quite a number of fires were already established prior to ND 929 starting its bombing run. Then, for the first time thus far in their short PFF career, the Luftwaffe decided to get seriously involved and 929 was attacked on three separate occasions by German night fighters. Initially 929 was attacked by a twin engine Ju88 night fighter. Despite the obvious temptation, Victor's training kicked in and he followed standard RAF procedure by not firing his guns, as the flashes from his weapons might well have helped identify their position to other fighters, and right now, dealing with one, was enough to keep them all occupied. Instead, at the appropriate moment, he called to John Forde, 'Corkscrew right!' as the bomb run was abandoned.

The Corkscrew was a very violent manoeuvre, designed to make it difficult, if not impossible for any following fighter to get a clear shot at his target. The call, 'Corkscrew right!' would bring an instant response from the pilot who would roll violently into the direction indicated by the gunner, as hard as his controls would permit, whilst at the same time forcing the nose down into a steep dive. After losing up to a thousand feet, the pilot would then haul the aeroplane round, reversing the turn and applying maximum 'g' force to bring the heavy aircraft into a maximum performance climb. The manoeuvre was usually successful not only in putting the enemy off his shot but also in enabling the Lancaster to disappear back into the dark night, unscathed.

Fortunately on this occasion the manoeuvre worked and they gave the Luftwaffe pilot the slip. Once safely back in the darkness, they orbited to starboard and were able gather their thoughts and recommence their bombing run at 8,600 feet. By the time they were over the remains of the marshalling yards, their colleagues ahead had stirred up dust and started fires that were now throwing up pillars of smoke to a height of 4–5,000 feet, pretty well obscuring most of the target. The Master Bomber instructed them to drop their ordnance on the centre of the fires. This they were able to do, and several hours later at debrief they found that the majority of their colleagues had done the same. The Master Bomber estimated they had achieved an impressive 90 per cent success rate.

But Victor still had work to do. Another German night fighter, this time a Messerschmitt Me110, found the opportunity to press home another attack. Again John Forde was able to throw it off the trail, and it appeared to have had enough for the time being. Unfortunately a third attack this time was by a fully radar equipped Me110. This one managed to get on their tail and made a strafing pass which peppered Victor's turret with cannon fire, slightly injuring him. It action also severed some hydraulic pipes putting the turret out of action and coating a now rather incensed Victor with hydraulic oil. Despite this, or maybe because of his intense annoyance, Victor was able to work with his pilot and get the plane manoeuvred so he could bring his guns to bear on the attacking German fighter and spray it with enough bullets to knock out its starboard engine. The Messerschmitt was last seen with its disabled engine fully ablaze, falling through the cloud undercast, apparently out of control.

There were few defences seen in the area apart from Victor's personal collection of night fighters, just a couple of odd searchlights and a sporadic amount of flak. Despite this low level of enemy action, for the second operation running, 35 Squadron lost a plane with ND620C-Charlie, the Kemp crew, failing to return. Again no one had seen or heard anything from ND620 since the time they had taken off. Two losses in two operations was a difficult situation for the new boys of 35 Squadron.

For his action that night Victor was recommended for an immediate award of the DFM (Distinguished Flying Medal) for his work in fending off the enemy fighters despite the adverse conditions he was confronted with.

## Louvain 11–12 May 1944

Victor's injuries were confirmed to be minor and just two days later he was heading back into Belgium aboard ND690C-Charlie with his usual crew on the way to Louvain and another railway marshalling yard complex. Louvain was some ten miles to the west of modern day Brussels Airport and so the round trip was once again less than three hours from chock to chock. They were designated a PFF Supporter for this raid. With their load of eighteen 500-lb GP bombs and a selection of TIs on board they took off from Graveley at 10.40 p.m. and headed south-east towards Brussels. It was a clear night and by 00.17 a.m. they were over Louvain peering through the light haze shrouding the target. On the run-in they had seen a huge explosion in the northern sector of the target area, where a previous crew had obviously got extra lucky with one of their bombs. The radio on C-Charlie had gone unserviceable on the way to target, but John Forde and his crew obviously felt they were sufficiently experienced by now and therefore confident enough to press on without it. Needless to say any additional instructions from the Master Bomber were simply not heard. They bombed from 7,000 feet but were unable to see their results of their efforts due to the increasing dust clouds kicked up, which further intensified the existing haze.

On the way home, they were aware of a huge fireball from the direction of Ghent. It was an odd situation, as it was far too late and somewhat far away from their planned route to be 'one of theirs'. Whether other RAF bomber crews were in action that night in the same area, no one knew. Alternatively it could have been some sort of sabotage action, an accident, or almost anything else for that matter, no one was sure. That said, if anyone did know anything about it, they were not prepared to record it during the 35 Squadron de-briefing that morning. Victor's plane had landed at 01.40 a.m. after one of their shortest sorties yet. More practice exercises followed, following the usual pattern used by the Pathfinders, to keep all the crews busy and sharp between operations.

# Duisburg 21–22 May 1945

Ten days after the raid on Louvain, the John Forde crew were again on the Order of Battle for 35 Squadron. This time they were leaving the railway system alone for a while and heading off to wreak havoc in the newly rebuilt industrial area of Duisburg, in the Ruhr Valley an area not only well known for the production of iron and steel and other engineering products, essential to Hitler's war effort, but also for the fearsome defences protecting the area. Somewhat cynically, because of the strength of these defences The Rhur valley was known amongst the bomber crews as Happy Valley.

Duisburg had taken a pounding just a year earlier and the war industry there had subsequently ground to a halt. However rapid rebuilding had put things back to rights and war goods were again flowing from the factories at full speed. Needless to say it had been decided in Whitehall that this was no longer acceptable and the flow had to be stopped once more, so the PFF would lead Bomber Command's attack to reverse the situation once again and to bring production to a halt.

On the Order of Battle for the raid of the 21st Victor's team were allocated Lancaster ND693H-How, for the night; it was to be their one and only flight in that particular plane. It was a big operation with 510 aircraft in the full bomber stream. As was usual by then, the first twenty or so aircraft in the bomber stream were the Mosquitos of the LNSF (Light Night Striking Force) and they flew along the intended route to target ahead of the main bomber stream, dropping Window at various points to confuse the German radar operators. Several of the Mosquitoes then left the main raid force and headed off to bomb alternate diversionary targets and to play further mind games with the German defenders and their co-ordinators. The Forde crew took off just a couple of minutes after 11.00 p.m. that evening and climbed out to 15,000 feet for the transit across the sea and into enemy territory. They had been designated a PFF Supporter and been allocated a bomb load of just one 4,000-lb Minol bomb, with the balance of the bomb bay taken up with a whole host of 1-lb incendiary devices. The cloud cover was completely 10/10ths for almost all of the way, and it remained so over the target. The plane's Air Speed Indicator (ASI) failed on the way to the target, just to help keep the flight deck crew on their toes. The Forde crew dropped their bomb load on its H2S picture and despite the cloud cover, their bomb's detonation was noted, and good photos obtained.

It was standard practice, once the bombs were dropped, to maintain height and heading until the bombs exploded. A camera then recorded the explosions so that the photo interpreters could then plot the accuracy of each individual aircraft as well as the overall accuracy of the raid. The effect of the incendiaries would no doubt have taken a while to produce the anticipated spread of fire and probably even longer to evaluate. Almost certainly it took the detailed work of the Photo Reconnaissance boys and girls some days to establish the full damage that was inflicted.

Other planes in the attack experienced problems including the loss of the Porter crew from 635 Squadron. This loss was the more poignant in that ND819, the

Porter Lancaster, was flying in the close company of three new 635 Squadron crews on their first ever Lancaster operation. It was hardly a morale-building experience for the novice crews. It was also noted that flak damage, an engine fire and brake loss further enlivened the night's work for the some of the other parts of the PFF contingent. The Forde crew had dropped its mixed load over Duisburg at 01.17 that morning, and were home safe in just one hour and fifty minutes from their 'time over target'.

## Dortmund 22–23 May 1944

The preoccupation with the enemy railway system obviously still featured highly in the minds of the PFF operational hierarchy as they planned the invasion of Europe, including the throttling of Hitler's supply lines. Just a couple of days later Victor and the rest of the Forde crew were allocated ND755 and asked to head off to Dortmund with fifteen other members of 35 Squadron and do the necessary damage to that city's rail marshalling yards. Dortmund was just 30 miles (or 10 to 15 minute flying time depending on the weather) to the east of their previous target, Duisburg, so the run was familiar and the flight time expected to be much the same, just a little longer. There were 361 bombers in the main bomber stream that night, and as was now becoming standard procedure they were led by fourteen LNSF Mosquitos tasked with dropping enough Window to confuse the enemy radar operators.

The target title 'Dortmund Railway Marshalling Yards' probably oversimplified that particular target area as it also encompassed a large north-south, east-west rail crossing point, the combination of marshalling yard, and a busy rail crossing point that almost certainly handled many thousands of tons of vital war materials on a daily basis. It was a significant target and to eliminate it was of great importance to both Bomber Command and the Allies' wider war effort. The standard load for the PFF Supporters that night was six of the regular 2,000-lb HE bombs.

Thus loaded with their six bombs, ND755 took off just after 10.45 p.m. and headed back to the Ruhr Valley. Severe icing was experienced at 17,000 feet and for some Lancaster crews it was bad enough to force them to turn back with damaged screens, broken aerials and other serious, game stopping problems. Victor and the Forde crew in 755 transited to target at 19,000 feet, thus avoiding the worst of the icing conditions and were over target at a couple of minutes short of 00.45. Their report indicated good marking and a neatly concentrated bombing run. Other planes reported slight flak, but the Forde crew made no mention of it. They returned to RAF Graveley at 02.56½. I guess to someone in the RAF administration system that half minute was of vital importance, but I'm not sure that Victor took a lot of notice.

It had not been a particularly good night for Bomber Command, although the target was pounded. The fleet lost eighteen crews in the course of that one operation, some 4.8 per cent of its number, including the Holman Crew in ND732 from 35

Squadron. Between operations the crews were now fully occupied with training flights, including an air test for the Forde crew on 21 May and a training sortie on 24 May, the very same day as their next raid. The PFF certainly expected their crews to be sharp and as up-to-speed as possible.

## Aachen 24–25 May 1944

The Allied planners were still in full railway mode when they allocated targets two days later. ND916F-Fox was Victor's new Lancaster and one that the Forde crew would use on and off for the next few weeks. This time they were heading for the marshalling yards on the northwest outskirts of the old university city of Aachen.

Aachen was just over the Belgian border near the Ardennes Forrest where the ill-fated Battle of the Bulge or Ardennes Counter Offensive as it was generally known to the Germans, was to take place in a little over six months' time. Again the Forde crew in 916 were designated a PFF Supporter's role and were loaded with the usual 4,000-lb Minol and sixteen 500-lb high explosive bombs.

Although not specifically mentioned by the records, this raid could well have been in two separate waves, as the Lancasters from 35 Squadron arrived over target at approximately 01.00. Other Pathfinder records show a second wave arriving a good half an hour later comprising just a relatively small number of Lancasters, estimated at between seventy and eighty aircraft. ND916 took off at 11.02 p.m. and was running in to target at exactly 01.00. They bombed on the red TIs as instructed by the Master Bomber and also appeared to score a direct hit on one of the green outer TIs and blow it to bits.

As with many of their earlier sorties, they were blessed with mainly clear skies with some light haze over the target, which of course mixed with a reasonable accumulation of smoke and dust for the late arrivals. The squadron reports again indicated neat pattern of bombing concentrations, tight on target. They were safely back down on the Graveley runway by 02.35.

## Bourg Leopold 27–28 May 1944

The Forde crew's tenth operation with 35 Squadron brought with it another step up the PFF ladder and on the raid on Bourg Leopold the Forde crew again in ND916F-Fox, were promoted to Illuminator. However, the post-raid report did not indicate what additional load (if any) was carried for this purpose, or what difference it made to the way they approached this particular operation. They were merely credited with a load of eight 1,000-lb high explosive bombs and a successful bombing run.

The Bourg Leopold target was Victor's first PFF raid specifically targeting the German military itself. The sortie was aimed at wiping out a complete barracks and camp complex on the eastern outskirts of the town named after the exiled Belgian King. In the far south west of the country, it was a mere five to ten minutes flying time for the Luftwaffe night fighters from the German border. Just thirteen Lancasters from 35 Squadron took part in this raid, as there were a number of other duties for the PFF force that night.

Victor took off a fraction after 00.30 and an hour and a half later, having swung lightly north of the target to avoid the civilian population in the town itself, started their bombing run into the barracks complex. Although in the mid-section of the PFF marking stream, the target area was very easily identified in the clear skies that night and they noticed that by the time they arrived over target, there were fires already starting to take hold in the south west corner of the barracks. By the time they had turned and were climbing *en route* for the coast, Victor with his Tail End Charlie prime viewing seat, noted that fires had started to spread over much of the area. The first bombs on this operation were dropped from 7,000 feet with the release height gradually increasing to some 13,000 feet for the last few Lancasters running in. There are no reports of any serious enemy defences in the area and by 04.00 Victor and his crew were taxiing back to their hardstand with their thoughts firmly on breakfast, little realising that just a few hours later they would be heading back in the opposite direction on another operation.

## Mardick 28–29 May 1944

The raid on Mardick, just south of Dunkirk appears to be the least successful and the least documented in Victor's flying career thus far. No reference is made in any Squadron report to a pinpoint target and there for once could well have been several main targets in the close proximity. What we do know was that it was all part of the plan to fool Hitler into thinking that Calais was the point for the forthcoming invasion.

There were significant port installations on the coast to choose from, including some Railway Marshalling Yards to the south and perhaps even the area around a medieval fort complex on the coast, almost certainly occupied by the German Military. That said, the close proximity to Dunkirk could also have thrown up a further possibility or two. Either way, the post-raid reports were not over encouraging, the target indicator system was either not used or certainly not seen and several reports indicated that the bombing was only 'fair' or in some instances seen dropping into the sea. Fortunately the Forde crew also registered a 'fair' for its bombing efforts and no 35 Squadron planes were lost on the operation. Some PFF Squadron crews cracked the two hours chock-to-chock time for the entire operation, Victor and the Forde crew missed it by one minute.

As Victor's crew did not appear on the Order of Battle for the next week, it seems fair to assume that they were granted seven days' leave to unwind and relax after a seriously intensive period of combat. It was on these occasions that Victor got to grab his train warrant and head back to see his family in Norwich. ND916 was then handed over to Squadron Leader Chidgey to use for his role as Deputy Master Bomber on the Operation on the 31 May that set out to successfully flatten the Trappes railway marshalling yards.

By then Victor's thoughts were elsewhere, the war could look after itself for a few days. It would still be there when he got back. However, the official paperwork he received that day when he returned from the Mardick operation advised him that from the next raid onward he would be flying as Flight Sergeant Victor Roe. For his Pilot, John Forde, however, it was a further major milestone in his life and a whole new world to embrace, as he used his leave to get married. Thus 6 June, D-Day, passed into history while the Forde crew enjoyed some well-earned leave.

## Forêt de Cerisy 7–8 June 1944

Forêt de Cerisy was a small forested area about four miles by six miles at its widest points some ten minutes' flying time inland from Omaha Beach. As the D-Day landings were just forty hours old the beaches and all roads inland would have been alive with soldiers and equipment. It was, of course D-Day plus one, and no doubt this would have been a major part of the briefing. It would have also been obvious to Victor as he had been allocated one of the best seats in the house to view the proceedings centred on the Normandy beaches, just 100 miles or so to the west.

If Victor could have spared the time for a quick glance down as ND916 raced overhead towards the target area he would have noticed the ground seething with activity. The aim of the raid was to destroy an ammunition dump buried deep in the heart of this woodland area. Other contemporary reports indicate that there was also a petrol dump located in the same area. Another Pathfinder squadron, 635 based at Downham Market, was tasked with obliterating the six-way road junction on the eastern edge of the same forested area. It would seem to make sense that this was a semi-combined operation to prevent any munitions or fuel escaping from the trap. Destroying it all where it was stored, as both raids were timed to take place at the same time would seem to have been eminently logical.

There were approximately thirty Lancasters in the combined PFF fleet. F-Fox had taken off from Graveley at 11.54 p.m. and again enjoyed clear skies with no flak or fighters to contend with. They arrived over target at 01.45 having approached from the west and dropped their eighteen 500-lb general purpose bombs on the green TI as instructed by the Master Bomber. They noted their bombing concentration seemed good, but also that there were other additional explosions about three miles away: that would have made complete sense with the boys from 635 Squadron hammering the associated road junction at the same time.

However it was not quite as straightforward as it sounds, as the Campbell crew in ND933S-Sugar were attacked by a lone German night fighter as they banked away from the target area. Victor was kept rather busy for the next ten to twenty minutes, scouring the inky skies for any signs of the lone defender returning. Fortunately it appeared that the Luftwaffe pilot decided against it. Either it seemed useless to press the attack on his own; perhaps he was running low on fuel or just simply lost sight of any of the targets in the darkness. Either way he was not heard from again that night and F/O Forde dropped them all safely back at base at 03.30½ precisely, according to the Intelligence Officer conducting the debrief following the raid.

Other crews with experienced pilots had earlier suggested that such minor anomalies in timing for the landings of their rookie colleagues could depend upon which bounce in the landing phase was counted … the first or the last. The talk in the mess and amongst the crew of 916 was not of this administrative variation but about the D-Day invasion and the Allies' successful return to mainland Europe. It would stay the main talking point across the airfield and in the bars of local pubs for many months yet.

## Fougères 8–9 June 1944

Once more, railway marshalling yards were back on the agenda for Victor and the Forde crew. This time the yards at Fougères in France some sixty miles inland from the Cherbourg Peninsula were marked by the navigator as their aiming point for the night. They were in ND696 on this occasion, with a bomb load of sixteen 500-lb general-purpose bombs and six 500-lb GP LD (general purpose, low drag bombs). This type of bomb apparently had better anti-personnel and concrete penetration characteristics and was also better suited against light armour than the more conventional bomb of a similar size.

The track out to Fougères was clear providing the Lancasters stayed below 7,000 feet, above that it was a full 10/10 cloud cover, comforting for the bomber crews to have available nearby to dodge into if German fighters were to appear, but fortunately on this occasion they didn't. Fougères seemed totally undefended so the suspicion was that all the Wehrmacht units in the area had been hurriedly moved forward to try to halt the invasion moving inland. The Forde de-brief noted that they had identified the target visually, dropped on the required TIs and cross confirmed the target with both the on board Gee Set and the H2S. There was no question in their mind that they had totally nailed it! Chock-to-chock times showed that 696E-Easy was airborne at 10.03 p.m. and back down by 02.58. Their time over target was just after 00.15. That was their thirteenth PFF operation out of the way and time to uncross their fingers.

## Rennes 9–10 June 1944

They were allocated ND692F-Fox for the next operation, and an additional Bomb Aimer, Flt Sgt Eyles. The two bomb-aimers almost certainly had complementary but separate jobs, Bill Eyles would be the visual bomb aimer if the weather was cooperating, leaving his opposite number, Bert Warner to bomb on the H2S when the weather was not so good. The system worked well. Several other crews were also allocated a second bomb aimer for this sortie, including the Master Bomber and the Deputy Master Bomber. This raid had all the ingredients of being something really different, as it was certainly something they had not attempted to do before. They were off to attack the Luftwaffe night fighter airfield at Rennes just to the south of the invasion zone. Some crews thought it somewhat reckless and a strategy akin to poking a nest of angry bees with a short stick, and something that may well backfire on them.

However, at the pre-operation briefing they were told that it would be in conjunction with three other raids on the airfields at Laval, Le Mans and Flers (the same Le Mans they had visited in their Halifax days). Thus the individual airfields would tend to be isolated and unable to call for assistance as every similar airfield in that sector would be in the same trouble. This tactical move was obviously aimed to severely weaken the support that these fighter bases could provide to the Wehrmacht ground troops attempting to defend against the southerly push of the Allied invasion force. This was a slightly longer raid that they had been used to in the recent weeks and they were airborne for almost four hours and twenty minutes. Fortunately there was little if any defensive action and the worst fears of the sceptics were completely unfounded. The Forde crew crossed the coast to the east of the invasion area and swept in to target from the east at 5,500 feet. On arrival the runways were clearly visible, or at least two of them were, but by the time they were heading home, most of the airfield was completely obliterated by smoke. They had taken off just before 00.30 and landed back at 04.50. Time over target was logged at just after 03.15. Bomb concentration was recorded as tight. They were obviously starting to get the hang of things.

## Lens 15–16 June 1944

Five days later the Forde crew were allotted ND936C-Charlie for their part of the planned obliteration of the railway marshalling yards at Lens. Lens was a coal mining area in the Pas de Calais, less than four miles from the location of the First World War battle site at Vimy Ridge and close to the Belgian border. Victor and all the aircrew on that operation had been made aware that Lens was a bit more important than a 'normal' raid. It was advised at the briefing that the Lens marshalling yards were the key to the main transport route out of the area. It was obviously critically important for the Nazis to ensure that they maintained the huge tonnage of coal flowing smoothly to their energy hungry war machine. To strangle this source of coal at Lens would be a very useful move for the Allied cause.

The Forde crew in C-Charlie were the second Lancaster airborne out of the seven planes from 35 Squadron allocated to the raid. There is no indication if such a small number was considered sufficient for the raid or if that was simply all that could be spared. Lancasters from 35 Squadron were also part of a second PFF contingent leading a raid on Fouillard the same night in support of the ground invasion forces. These were indeed busy times for RAF Graveley. C-Charlie got airborne just after 11.30 a.m. and was back at base less than three hours later. Unsurprisingly their recorded 'time over target' was noted at 12.52. Seventy-eight minutes to take off and get to target, ten minutes to unload, and seventy-eight minutes to turn round and get back to base. Their bombing had again been concentrated on the TIs and C-Charlie reported two huge explosions in the target area about a minute apart as they ran in to deliver their bombs.

## Sterkrade 16–17 June 1944

It was almost as if they were being asked to play catch-up with the rest of 35 Squadron, as they found out they were being assigned an old friend ND916F-Fox for the operation against Sterkrade on the night of the 16 June. On this raid, it was an even smaller group of just three Lancasters that were assigned from 35 Squadron to this raid, all were designated Visual Backers-up. Just to add to that new scenario, their bomb load was different than before. They were not only loaded with the standard 4,000-lb GP bomb but were also carrying twelve 500-lb GPTDs (high explosive bombs with time delay mechanisms). All three of the squadron's planes again carried an additional Bomb Aimer, indicating they now all had H2S to assist them. They were once again operating over reasonably familiar territory on this occasion as they were back along the Ruhr Valley, just a few miles from Duisburg and Essen, the sites of two of their earlier PFF operations.

This time it was the Sterkrade-Holton synthetic oil plant that was the subject of their undivided attention when they ran in to target just after 01.15 a.m. that following morning. Under the protection of a total cloud cover at 12,000 to 14,000 feet, they bombed from 18,000 feet through the cloud on to the TI's glow. Many bomb flashes were reported and Victor was treated to the heartening sight the glow from many large fires growing in intensity as their plane roared away from the target area. The Sterkrade plant was obviously a serious priority target for the Allies as it was singled out for further close attention from the RAF, and also from a one off attack by the B24s and B17s of USAAF during their massive daylight missions.

The Forde Crew were not on the Order of Battle for the best part of a week, though naturally the crew were not putting their feet up during that time. They had some daylight cross-country training mixed with gunnery and bomb aiming practice on the following Sunday, Monday and Tuesday. Then on the Thursday morning they conducted an exercise involving Fighter Affiliation and bombing. On their return to Graveley they had a bite to eat and few hours' rest, prior to the briefing for their next training sortie that same evening. Each of these sorties was in the order of two hours long, longer than some of their actual operations against the enemy.

## Laon 22–23 June 1944

The Laon railway marshalling yards were the designated target for the raid on the night of the 22–23 June. Laon was some seventy-five miles to the north east of Paris, fairly close to the Belgian border.

The Forde crew was allocated ND929L-Love for the night and designated a PFF Illuminator for this trip. As an Illuminator they had aboard a dual load of ordnance, some for lighting, and some for bombing. It was a fresh experience. Needless to say this involved taking two runs at the target, one to deliver the flares for the illumination, the second a short time later to drop the bomb load. On the first run in they were scheduled to drop the twenty-four hooded flares, after which they were expected to orbit the target area and run in again at much the same height and much the same angle, to release their bomb load of 5,000 lb of high explosives. At 00.59 they ran in to target at 11,500 feet and released the illuminator flares, then holding height at 11,300 feet they orbited the target area and came round again on a similar track some six minutes later to drop their HE bombs. All those hours of training had at last come together; this was the full PFF involvement they had been working towards for months.

The raid appeared good, though reports varied on the amount of collateral damage to the town that closely surrounded the yards. They taxied off the runway at 02.50, job done.

## Middel Straëte 24–25 June 1944

Their operation originated by Bomber Command two days later, was to destroy the V1 site at Middel Straëte in the Pas de Calais some six miles from the Belgian border. The closeness of the site ensured a swift return for the 35 Squadron, with L-Love taking a mere one hour fifty minutes from take-off to touchdown.

Although it was an altogether much shorter affair, it was a small site and so the PFF were needed to pinpoint the target. That said it seems that it was still somewhat difficult to mark. It appears from the post raid de-briefing there was a reasonable scatter in the bombing pattern, although that may be attributed to the need for a more carpet-bombing approach for a very small target.

Another plane in the attack formation noted a huge white explosion that coincided perfectly with the bomb run from Victor's crew. It may well be they were the crew that got lucky. Some miles south, the same night, another squadron from the PFF was also giving its full and undivided attention to the rocket site at Le Grand Rossignol. Just twenty-four hours later the V1 site at Liegescourt was marked out for a similarly devastating attack by the Pathfinders.

The feeling in the mess that week was that they were actually starting to get somewhere and almost certainly making a difference.

## Oisemont / Neuville-au-Bois 27–28 June 1944

This target is noted by two names, depending on which squadron records are read. Either way, it was the German's V1 construction site close to the French villages of Oisemont and Neuville-au-Bois that was the focus of the Pathfinder's attention that night. The fact that there was just a field or two between the last house in one village and the first in the next, may well explain the name confusion. Crews from 35 Squadron got round this by using both names together in their reports and logbooks.

However, it appears that it was a hugely important site in the eyes of the Allied Commanders and as such it was visited on no less than five occasions, four times by the RAF and once by the USAAF. The RAF came calling on 20, 23 and 30 June and then finally on 1 July. In the middle of this RAF campaign the boys from the USAAF were given their turn with a daylight raid on 21 June. On the last RAF raid in June, Bomber Command had mustered 761 planes loaded with a little over three thousand tons of ordnance. The whole area resembled a badly ploughed field by the time the sun rose the following morning, and there was still one more attack being planned.

As Oisemont was situated just inland in the Pas de Calais area, it was always going to be another very short raid and ND929's efforts that night added a mere two hours fifteen to Victor's logbook. They took off at 00.22 and had their first experience of being the very last plane to leave RAF Graveley that night. Looking at the order of Battle of other PFF Squadrons, they may well have also been the last PFF Lancaster to bomb Oisemont that night, before the full might of the Main Bomber Stream arrived. The Forde crew reported a 3/10 cloud cover as they ran in to target at 01.30. It looked to Victor as if they had achieved a good bombing concentration and after an uneventful return flight they were back down on the ground and taxiing in shortly after 02.30.

There was just one more non-operational cross-country for the Forde crew on the 30 June lasting exactly one hour, before the calendar in the mess was flipped over a page to July and High Summer 1944 was upon them. Even with British Double Summertime in place, the nights were now starting to draw in. It was probably fair to say that the Forde Crew were so busy they hardly noticed.

# 6

# Operations—July–October 1944

### Oisemont/Neuville-au-Bois 1 July 1944

For the first time in their tour of duty, the Forde crew in ND702E-Easy were allocated an immediate return visit to the scene of their previous raid. The V1 Flying Bomb construction site at Oisemont/Neuville-au-Bois was apparently not flattened quite as much as the tacticians at Bomber Command felt necessary, so a fifth and final allocation of high explosives were detailed for the completion of the job. 35 Squadron were designated part of the delivery system. The Forde crew were also promoted to the big league as they were designated Deputy Master Bomber, for this raid.

There was no question of just running to target, dropping bombs and then heading back home. This time their assignment was to orbit high above the target area to support the Master Bomber, Squadron Leader Cranswick, who had taken off from Graveley just one minute ahead of Victor's team. The crew of E-Easy saw the target visually as well as being able to identify it on Gee, but they had had such a good flight out to the Pas de Calais that they actually arrived ahead of the Master Bomber and had to orbit above the target area for a while until he turned up to put his plan into action. However, the scattered cloud was making it difficult for the first wave of PFF Bombers to see the TIs. Some crews could see them but others were having real problems. Some bombed on their Gee set's data and others were given the order 'Square Mile' by the Master Bomber, which had the effect of at least getting the majority of the bombs in the general area of the target, which by then was almost unrecognisable as anything in particular, never mind a sophisticated weaponry construction site.

The post-raid reconnaissance photos show a moon-like landscape with literally hundreds, if not thousands of interlinking craters of chalky sub-soil covering ninety per cent of the target area surface. This time they were airborne for two hours and forty-five minutes, and although they were second aircraft away, they were almost last to get home, only the Master Bomber and a couple of stragglers arriving as they were taxiing back to their hard stand. It was 03.15.

Theoretically, Victor and the rest of John Forde's crew had a rest day on Sunday 2 July, but as with most PFF stations, the general principle of rest days were frowned upon and unsurprisingly a practice exercise of formation flying was sorted for those crews not on combat operations that day. To add to the interest, Victor was given his brief moment in the sun with a short session of air-to-sea gunnery practice.

## Villeneuve-Saint-Georges 6–7 July 1944

This time they were back to one of their regular targets, the railway marshalling yard complexes that helped feed the Nazi war machine. Villeneuve-St-Georges was one of the bigger rail yards serving Orly Airport and an area to the south of Paris. It was located just across the River Seine from the airport and covered a large 'T' shaped area roughly two miles by two miles at its widest points. It also had more than its fair share of locomotive repair sheds scattered about the site. Knocking it out would be a significant achievement. Victor's crew were still in 702 following their successful raid on Oisemont, but this time they were allocated the job of PFF Illuminator. As such the first section of their ordnance load was twenty-four hooded flares, and the main bomb load eight 1,000-lb bombs, two of which were the LD variants. Being an Illuminator would again mean making two passes over the target, the second of which would be when the local defenders were awake, fully alert, almost certainly rather annoyed and trigger happy.

They were the very last plane away on this operation and followed the two Backer-up planes of the Cranswick and Lambert crews. Sadly both Backer-up planes were lost on this operation. Once they had taken off and signed off from Graveley tower, they were never heard from again. So after several loss-free sorties over a few weeks, 35 Squadron suddenly lost two experienced crews in a single night.

Understandably Victor was not to know that until he returned to Graveley at 03.40 the next morning. Having taken the first trip over the target to drop the hooded flares at 01.12, they then orbited and returned six minutes later to make their bombing run. Reports from the crews indicated a successful operation with the repair sheds taking a particularly heavy pounding. As Victor's plane ran into target, the boys in the cockpit noted a larger than normal fireball from the target area. It seemed that one of the crews a minute or two ahead of them in the bomber stream had just got lucky. However, when they returned to base and heard about their own losses, they suddenly realised that that fireball could quite easily have been the final moments of one of 35 Squadron's own missing aircraft. It was a sobering thought.

## Marquise/Mimoyecques 6 July 1944

The raid on Mimoyecques the early morning of 6 July was one of the few daylight raids at that time for 35 Squadron and at one hour and fifty-five minutes also one of the shortest. Despite this it was probably one of the most important ever undertaken by Victor and the John Forde crew. Mimoyecques was a most heavily reinforced bunker complex built to house Hitler's V3 Supergun. The V3 was the third of the Nazi's, so called, Vengeance Weapons. This monster gun constructed by the giant Krupp works was being built to throw 310-lb shells at over 160 kilometres per hour, across the English Channel at London. It was designed to be yet another decisive blow to bring England to its knees. It was housed in the old Hidrequent limestone quarry at Mimoyecques under a five-metre thick overlaying protective concrete dome, in a building designed on similar lines to the notorious V2 bunkers. It would be an extremely tough position to crack and special ordnance and expertise would be needed.

What Bomber Command had planned was the marking and 'softening up' of the Mimoyecques site by Victor and the PFF boys, then have 617 Squadron (The Dambusters) follow them in with a selection of the Barnes Wallace designed 12,000-lb 'Tallboy' bunker penetrating bomb. Fortunately for the Allies this one raid hit the site very hard and due to the near total destruction it caused at Mimoyecques, the installation and the Supergun programme never progressed to full completion. In fact the raid set back the programme so far that the production of further examples of the V3 was slowed and then finally halted in mid-project when war materials ceased to flow through Europe as the rail system was pounded to a halt. This overwhelming disruption to the movement of men and materials was later analysed as being almost entirely due to the nightly raids by PFF and Bomber Command on the European railway marshalling yard network. It was a comment that would have made Victor and his crew smile with satisfaction.

Once more they were in ND702G-George, and for the second time in their PFF career they were allocated the position of Deputy Master Bomber. Again, they arrived over the target area before the Master Bomber, and also apparently behind the main force. TIs and bombs were already raining down with some effect, and the Master Bomber dropped fresh markers and tidied the bomb patterns up still further. One stick of bombs that originally appeared to be slightly astray was actually seen to be clustered on or around the entrance tunnel to the complex, so it appeared a rather lucky bonus was scored by one of the PFF team. A further heartening sight for the Master Bomber and his Deputy was a large reddish explosion as they were leaving the area; someone had obviously hit a particularly sensitive part of the bunker complex.

For the Forde Crew, it was not quite such a trouble free run, as the Ack-Ack guns in the area were taking aim on the bombers while they flew in on their bomb runs. ND702 was hit three times by flak. Fortunately this produced no injuries to the crew, and no significant damage to the aircraft. Just after 09.10 they touched down at Graveley, ready for de-brief and breakfast. ND702 was handed back to the ground crew for a thorough check and a few cosmetic repairs.

After a pretty short day on the sixth, they had another formation flying exercise the following day, again with a spell of air-to-air gunnery for Victor to let loose with

his guns from the back of the plane. With a start at10.50, just over an hour in the
air and back to the mess for dinner, it was a lifestyle they all felt they could get used
to. Not a bad work schedule, especially when they heard they were stood down
until the Sunday afternoon. At that stage of Victor's RAF career, it was proving to be
quite a convenient war, all things considered.


## Caen D-Day Landing Support 7 July 1944

For the first time the records show that Victor volunteered for an extra duty and
flew with a different team other than the John Forde crew. For this raid, organised
in double quick time to support the Allied ground troops as they pushed forward
from the Normandy beachheads, he was with the P. J. Bryant crew in ND646. It
was also a major first for them all, in that they knew before they took off that they
had been tasked to bomb open fields as part of the raid. Nevertheless as this was all
part of the very specific requirement of the commanders on the ground, and it was
done with the same professionalism as any other PFF target. For sure it raised the
odd wry smile amongst colleagues and a few ribald post-raid comments in the mess,
which was inevitable. Nonetheless it was an action that the Army thought would
help loosen up the German's faltering hold on that part of France, and after all that
it what it was all about.

They had a 13,000-lb bomb load for this trip, as did most of the attacking aircraft,
and they were accompanied by a really impressive fighter cover to see them safely
there and back. Their route was understandably straight over the beaches where the
Allies already had a foothold and a short run to target inland.

ND646 recorded its 'Bombs Gone' time just twelve seconds before that of
ND928, with both planes flying at something in excess of 100 miles an hour. It
was obviously a pretty crowded piece of sky, even for the experienced PFF crews.
After this trip, Victor and his team encountered another Intelligence Officer keen
on absolute accuracy in their de-brief. Thus that day when the times for 646 were
logged in the Squadron Records, the officer recorded:

> Take-off 20.46½.
> Time over target 22.23.30.
> Landed 23.45½ .


## Les Catelliers 9 July 1944

The raid on the V1 sites and their supply dumps was now a top priority and Les
Catelliers, just twenty miles inland from Le Havre, was the next of many that the
Pathfinder Force were tasked to eliminate. It was really odd or at least must have

felt so for the crews involved for several interlinking reasons, starting with the fact that there were just two crews detailed from 35 Squadron; The Hoover crew in ND936C-Charlie as Master Bomber and The Forde Crew, back in ND702G-George as Deputy Master Bomber. All the other reasons flowed from this. They took off within a minute of each other and landed almost three hours later, with the same one-minute spacing in their arrival times. Their bomb loads were identical, containing the majority of pyrotechnics and just six HE Bombs to get the raid off to a positive start.

The target indication appeared good, but the accuracy of the main bomber stream was a little more scattered than had been hoped for, despite the best efforts and instructions of the Master Bomber. It would be fair to mention here that a further contingent of bomb crews from 35 Squadron were dispatched the same day to mark the raid on yet another V1 storage facility at L'Hay, so the rest of the Squadron at RAF Graveley was also working at combat level and not on a rest day. The Flying Bomb launch sites and their supply dumps were the PFF target of choice.

## Nucourt 10 July 1944

The next on the list of places to visit for Victor and his crew were the caves at Nucourt where the Nazis had hidden reserves of V1 Flying Bombs and a supporting quantity of spares. It was the target for the early morning raid on Monday 10 July, and was given the name Operation Crossbow. Nucourt was about fifteen minutes flying time beyond the target at Les Catelliers, so for the crews of 35 Squadron it was over reasonably familiar ground. Once again it had the additional bonus in that a considerable amount of the run was over friendly, Allied held, territory.

They coasted in near Le Havre and flew along the river valley to the target area. The Forde Crew were again in 702G-George and took off second in a stream of twelve 35 Squadron Lancasters. They were then to meet up with twelve other PFF 635 Squadron Lancasters from Downham Market while *en route* to target. There was a lot of cloud over the target area and the majority of the bomber stream bombed on the data from their on board H2S and Gee systems. The bombing accuracy and results were also hard to estimate because of the cloud cover and it would take the later reconnaissance flights to collect this information. All 35 Squadron crews returned, although some bursts of heavy flak were reported in the target area. The Blakey crew, in 929 for this operation, had a failure on their Gee box, but rather than bring their bombs back, were a bit opportunist and tucked in tight behind another Lancaster on its run in to target and used its bomb release timing to drop their own load.

True to form, their 'day off' on the 11 July was livened up by two separate highlights. The first was the news that John Forde had been promoted and was now Flight Lieutenant. The second, but less dramatic event was that they were given a bombing exercise to carry out. They were tasked with a one and a half hour trip to a bombing range, and this short trip allowed the Forde crew to keep ND702 until the following day when they were back on the Order of Battle.


## Rollez 12 July 1944

Victor and the Forde crew stayed with ND702G-George for their next trip across to Europe, and just for a change it was an afternoon raid to the Flying Bomb site at Rollez in the Pas de Calais. To head off on a sortie just after lunch and be back in time for dinner was thought by all to be a most civilised way of conducting a war and met with the full approval of the Forde crew. To ease matters further they were designated as PFF Bombers for this sortie and a selection of the LNSF Mosquitos were tasked with doing the target marking. That way the 35 Squadron Lancasters were all able to transit to the target area, complete the bomb run and return home at a pretty safe height of 16,000 feet.

All six of the planes from RAF Graveley had an identical ordnance load comprising of sixteen 500-lb GPTD bombs and two 500-lb GPLD bombs. The results all appeared to be good and most of the crews were reported to have bombed on the release of ordnance by the lead Pathfinder Mosquito which was fitted with the latest Oboe navigation system. That was as accurate as you could get.

The Forde crew were indeed back at RAF Graveley by 4.20 p.m., which allowing for a normal de-brief still gave them sufficient time for a drink in the mess before dinner.


## Les Landes Vielles et Neuves 15 July 1944

The Les Landes V1 site was about twenty miles inland from the Channel coast and some twelve miles south of their earlier target of Oisemont. There were again just two crews sent from 35 Squadron on this sortie. In L933, the W/Cdr Whenham crew as Master Bomber and in PB183, the Forde crew as Deputy Master Bomber. As on previous occasions when just a couple of 35 Squadron crews were singled out for a raid, many of the other Graveley crews were tasked with an alternative operation. On this occasion the PFF Lancasters of 35 Squadron paid a return trip to the V1 flying bomb supply dump at Nucourt. As with the first raid, they were in the company of the Downham Market based crews of 635 Squadron.

The target area was obscured with ten-tenths cloud cover when Victor arrived; both the Master Bomber and John Forde could see that the TIs dropped by the PFF Mosquitos were still faintly visible through the cloud. Unfortunately neither of them considered their residual brightness sufficiently strong for bombing purposes, so the main bomber stream was given the order to 'Square Mile'. This in fact was the technical order to the crews to rely on their on-board instruments or any visual clues they could latch on to successfully complete their bomb run. The results were bound to be uncertain. The Forde crew were airborne at 00.44 and back at Graveley by 03.14.

## St Philibert 16 July 1944

St Philibert was yet another of the V1 associated sites that were the mainstay operations for most of the crews of 35 Squadron, during those warm weeks of high summer 1944. Looking through the Squadron records compiled at the de-briefing by the Intelligence Officer, the dominant data reported on is the trial use of bombing in a three-ship V- (or Vic) formation. It appears that the Oboe equipped Mosquitos led the raid in and the following PFF Lancasters followed them in waves of three in V-formation.

The consensus was that the Mosquito was a bit quick and that the formation was very difficult to hold, particularly as the lead plane, Victor and the Forde crew, were simply unable to coax their plane to generate the required speed to stay with the Mosquito, and as such the V-formation simply fell away. Another plane in the first few waves had already lost an engine, so that too was unable to keep up the speed set by the Mosquito. It was all part of the learning curve for the Pathfinders as they strove to improve their techniques.

The other most notable change that became evident that day was in the Squadron entries. What appears to be an extremely pedantic Operations Officer had started introducing a new pattern of recording all aircraft times to within a quarter of a minute or in the equivalent in seconds, or a combination of both. According to official records the Forde crew returned to Graveley at seventeen and three quarter minutes after five o'clock, with their time over target given as four minutes past four, plus twenty seconds. Thus Victor's operation to attack the St Philibert target started at twenty-three and a quarter minutes past two that afternoon, with two more of 35 Squadron's Lancasters a mere fifteen seconds and thirty seconds behind them.

This extreme closeness of take-off times could be accounted for by the fact that the bomb loads allocated to each of the planes for this raid was for once not uniform or consistent. Records show that each plane seemed to have a totally different weight of ordnance aboard, which would no doubt have altered their take off characteristics and speeds. It is not certain that either the Control Tower or the Station CO would be happy with such close proximity on the runway, certainly when it was not an operational requirement. All three would have been rolling at much the same time and a tyre blowout or engine failure on the lead plane (Victor's) at high speed, half way through a take-off run, would have almost certainly produced an accident of catastrophic proportions.

This in fact had happened some short time before on an American base very close to RAF Graveley. They too were equipped with heavy bombers, the Boeing B-17s. An incident on the take-off roll produced a concertina effect with several fully loaded planes colliding and exploding with their entire ordnance loads. The damage inflicted on that occasion was so vast that the first repair crew on scene were allocated the task of building a road down to the bottom of the crater so the rest of the team could start the reconstruction work! The hole was that deep. The PFF Mosquitos were known to take off fairly close together, but being a much smaller plane their pilots took alternative sides of the runway centre line to give each aircraft's crew a sporting chance if things ahead of them went a bit awry during the take-off roll.

Most of 35 Squadron's planes had returned before 5.30 p.m., so once again the crews had the opportunity of a quick beer before dinner.

## Forêt de Nieppe 31 July–1 August 1944

Twenty miles inland from Dunkirk, this Flying Bomb site was the next in line for a concentrated attack by Bomber Command in the overnight period between the two main summer months. The Forde crew was one of five 35 Squadron Lancasters flying this particular overnight sortie, and had again been allocated the Deputy Master Bomber role. Unfortunately the target area was totally cloud covered down to 2,000 feet and although marker flares, TIs and bombs were dropped it was just impossible for any crew to note the effects of their night's work.

The Osmond crew in ND690, who were immediately behind Victor were hit several times with flak but survived. The Marsden crew had a mechanical failure with their plane's bomb release mechanism and were devastated at having to bring their bomb load all the way back to Graveley unused, despite going round and having a second attempt at getting the ordnance to release over target. It was not the best of nights for 35 Squadron.

## Bois de Casson 3 August 1944

Bois de Casson, just outside Paris was the next V1 site on the target list, and this daylight raid was carried out more in line with how the text books recommended and as such it appeared to be a far better raid than the Forêt de Nieppe trip, just two days earlier. It was one of three raids on Flying Bomb sites that day and Bomber Command had managed to amass 1,114 planes to share the load of the three targets. It was the biggest single set of raids directed at V1 sites, thus far in the war.

The other raids that day were at Trossy St Maxim and a return trip to finish off the Forêt de Nippe site. 35 Squadron were also called upon to help mark the Trossy raid.

As you might reasonably expect, Bois de Casson was embedded in woodland, and was believed to be mainly a storage site, but nevertheless a target well worth eliminating. The Forde crew were allocated a Backer-up role again, and as such carried eight Yellow TIs and six 1,000 lb bombs. The estimates of cloud over target reported by the different crews varied between 2/10 and 5/10 Cumulus with tops extending to well over 10,000 feet, which is quite a variation for the twenty to thirty minutes the raid took to complete.

Surprisingly there were enough gaps between the clouds to enable all crews to report good visibility over target. As expected the Master Bomber got his markers down precisely on target. With the target nicely set up the Forde crew and others in the PFF team were able to replicate the Master Bomber's earlier accuracy and the following PFF Lancasters and the main bomber stream were able to continue the good work. There were no fighters encountered over the target area, but the flak was reported as quite heavy and scored quite a number of hits on the incoming aircraft. It was noted that a wave of Halifax bombers in the main bomber stream seemed to be badly mauled, though they all appeared to survive, drop their load and head for home. At least one PFF Lancaster was seen to take a hit and start its return journey with just three of its Merlins working.

The reports for Victor's crew were much as expected. Take-off time was 12.24, and gave them a time over target of 14.02. 15.24 was their recorded time for touchdown back at Graveley, well in time for the operation de-brief and a spot of afternoon tea if they felt so inclined. However I suspect a shower and a beer in the mess was more to their liking.

The twinned raid to Trossy had fared much worse and encountered heavy, well-aimed flak. 35 Squadron's companions on this raid, 635 Squadron, lost two very experienced crews, the Massey crew (Deputy Master Bomber) and the Bazalgette crew. The Massey crew had the tail of their plane blown completely off by flak, and the Bazalgette crew had both starboard engines hit and set ablaze. Despite the tremendous damage to his aircraft, Bazalgette persisted with his attack and accurately marked the target. Neither plane stood a chance and Bazalgette died in the subsequent crash. For his efforts on this raid, Bazalgette was awarded the VC.

## Bec d'Ambès 4 August 1944

Bec d'Ambès was the location of a major fuel refinery plant on the Atlantic seaboard of France and was essential to the Nazis for the provision of petrol for the Panzer and other mechanised units supporting the defence to the Allies invasion and liberation of France. For the fourth trip in a row, ND702G-George was allocated to the Forde Crew, along with the Deputy Master Bomber role on the sortie.

It was unfortunately a total disaster for Victor's crew as G-George developed such a serious malfunction with the rudder trim that they were forced to return to base after less than an hour into the operation. Somehow the connection to the rudder trim actuator stretched and became inoperative and even with full aileron trim applied to counter this John Forde was unable to keep the Lancaster flying straight and level. They had to turn back. They kept their TIs, but jettisoned the bombs safely and returned to base just after 15.15 p.m. Needless to say this raid was not going to count towards their operations' tally.

The only good news from the raid was that there were two Deputy Master Bombers allocated to the raid, so it could still go ahead at full strength, and the remaining planes had the bonus of clear skies over target. This meant the whole operation was pretty successful and succeeded in cutting off a major fuel supply route to the German front line. It greatly hampered the defenders who were positioned in the path of the Allies push towards Paris and the south. Further south still in France that same day, the fuel storage tanks at Pauillac also got the full Pathfinder treatment and were extremely badly mauled.

In that one day, the German fuel supplies in Western France took a devastating knock from which they would never recover.

## Forêt de Nieppe 6 August 1944

The Ground crews at 35 Squadron weaved their usual magic on 702 and Victor and the rest of the Forde crew were very soon able put the trim problem behind them. This meant on Sunday 6 August, just before lunch they were already back aboard ND702 and heading back towards the Forêt de Nieppe to have a final go at finishing off what was left of the V1 supply depot that they had visited a week earlier. They were once again assigned the Deputy Master Bomber role.

It was hazy over target when they arrived at 01.04 a.m. The main bomber force took some careful nurturing by the Master Bomber to unload their bombs as he directed, but after a while he manage to get some semblance of order and accuracy into the attack. Looked at overall the raid was deemed successful, even if it had a somewhat scattered grouping by the main force in its earlier phase.

702G-George was loaded with a mixture of yellow TIs and six 1,000-lb high explosive bombs. They bombed from 9,500 feet, at 01.01 a.m., running in on target on a track that was virtually due south. They touched down at Graveley at 02.04 a.m., after a mere two hours twenty-three minutes airborne.

## Totalize 7–8 August 1944

An alternative and more formal title for this operation was Normandy Battle Area A/P numbers 4 and 5. It basically entailed sections of Bomber Command pitching in to help with the ground offensive. What they had been asked to do was bomb the main German defensive line to loosen the hold of the Wehrmacht ground forces on their positions. This was intended to enable the Allied troops to move forward quicker and in a way that they took fewer casualties.

The Forde crew were once again in their regular Lancaster ND702G-George and were designated as Backer-up. It was another raid that started just before midnight and finished just after midnight. Total operation time was a mere one hour thirty-five minutes … a much shorter time airborne than some of the previous training exercises they had flown.

There were six main blockage points pinpointed by the ground commanders and each of these was allocated a senior PFF crew to mark and lead the bombing on that section of the front. Victor's crew were allotted a dozen red marker TIs and just two 1000-lb MCT bombs. These were the type that triggered instantly, thus spreading the blast through 360 degrees before it penetrated the ground thus 'wasting' some of its devastating blast available by blowing a deep crater. It was a really nasty piece of ordnance, but totally ideal for causing havoc and mass injuries amongst fields full of infantry without any means of protection.

Again they followed the standard attack route by coasting in overhead the Allied held beaches and territory and bombed a short distance ahead of the advancing invasion troops. The 35 Squadron post-raid reports indicated a success, but in some ways it was going to be difficult to achieve anything further after the initial wave. It was called off by the Master Bomber once the dust, dirt and smoke from the first wave of the attack was felt to be obscuring things too much and in all probability little more could be achieved at that time. It is fair to say Victor was back in his hut and asleep at a time no later than he would have been after a good 'lads' night out' on an off-duty day.

## Forêt de Nieppe 9–10 August 1944

For this second raid on the V1 installations in the Forêt de Nieppe area, the Forde crew, once again in ND702G-George, was designated PFF Master Bomber. Their success in earlier raids had been recognised and now they had made it to the very top of the tree in the Pathfinder Force, and were now being tasked with the job of primary marker for getting the raid started and for orchestrating any changes it needed whilst it was all unfolding beneath them.

For this role they were loaded with twenty-four marker flares and eight 1,000-lb bombs. The post-raid reports indicated that the marking was good, but initial bombing a bit scattered. A further mid-raid drop of green markers seemed to tighten up the bomb concentration and at least one large, white explosion was noticed while the crews from 35 Squadron were still in the area. No doubt Victor would have enjoyed his usual grandstand seat for viewing these pyrotechnics on the way home.

There were further smiles all round in the Forde crew on the 10 August when it was learned that Bert Warner and John Rollins had also been promoted and they too had followed John Forde to the rank of Flight Lieutenant. As they were on the Order of Battle the next day, there is no record if the celebrations were muted, postponed, or if they all simply flew the next operation with a serious hangover.

## Douai 11 August 1944

By now the rear gun turret of G-George was becoming Victor's second home, and the daylight raid to obliterate the railway marshalling yards at Douai was no exception.

Douai was just about five minutes flying time on from one of their earlier raids to the yards at Lens in Northern France. It was very close to the Belgian border and very familiar combat territory to the Forde crew and many of the PFF crews. On this occasion there would be a nine-ship contingent from 35 Squadron. They also were briefed that their colleagues in 635 Squadron would also be in the area at the time as they were going with them, but would peel off at Lens and give that yard a further beating, just in case anyone had thought of trying to repair it and bring it back into the war.

They were again designated as Master Bomber, for the operation and 702's bomb bay was loaded with a standard mix of TIs and high explosive bombs. It was another of those extremely civilised operations that they were getting used to, where they left Graveley just after lunch and were back later in the afternoon, well in time for a beer before dinner.

For once the weather was kind to them as they approached the yards, and the 3/10 cloud cover was broken enough for them to visually identify the target and mark it accurately for the following aircraft. In fact the Squadron records recorded the marking as, 'bang on', pretty high praise for a novice Master Bomber in the official reporting jargon of the day.

However, things were not quite so good for those following the first wave in, as the accuracy of the marking and subsequent tight bombing pattern meant that the concentration of smoke and dust created was once again very high in the target area. The majority of the following Lancaster crews had no option but to bomb on the TIs, as all else on the ground was totally obscured by the time they arrived just a few minutes later. Victor was back at Graveley by 05.15 a.m., and all the crews returned safely around the same time. It was almost a copybook operation.

With the war in such a critical phase there was no time for Victor or his fellow crewmates to rest on their laurels, as they soon found out when they were advised that they were on the Battle Order for the following night's operation. This time they were back off to Germany.

## Rüsselsheim 12-13 August 1944

Rüsselsheim-am-Main was the home to the Adam Opel AG motor works. It was a pre-war motor car plant, now fully engaged in producing military trucks and aircraft parts including engines, fuselages and cockpits. Obviously it was a prime candidate for the close attention of Bomber Command and its well-proven PFF led pattern of bombing.

Situated between Frankfurt to the east and Wiesbaden to the west and beside a very distinctive section of the River Rhine, it should have been easily identified, but it wasn't. The de-brief report from the Forde crew, acting as Primary Visual Marker, commented that the target area simply wasn't visual. A combination of cloud cover, ground haze, searchlight glare and some markers that had been dropped blind, made the whole thing impossible to unravel and positively pin point the target.

Victor's team were once again in ND702, but on this trip had an addition pilot on board, F/O Douglas. They heard the Master Bomber instructing to 'drop on whites', but by then they had turned round and were already many miles away on the homeward leg of the flight. John Forde had already decided the whole thing was a complete waste of time and ordnance and had elected to come home and returned with their bomb load intact. They had already wasted fuel, time and nervous energy; they might as well at least retain the bombs for a better day.

Others, however, held different views and decided they would drop their load 'somewhere', but what markers there were, were very scattered and some reports even mention the main river being visual at the time, and that was a good few miles to the west of the target. It was altogether a pretty unsuccessful operation made worse by the loss of the Henderson crew from another PFF unit and several reported losses from the main bomber stream; a night for them all to forget. There were several isolated fires on or around the site, but nothing of any major size or significance.

## Falaise 14 August 1944

The Falaise Gap (or 'Stalingrad in the West' in Wehrmacht-speak) and its implications for the way the Nazi hierarchy totally misread the situation and then misdirected their military actions in Normandy has been the subject of books, lectures and discussion papers for many decades following the campaign. It was of course still unfolding on the ground as Victor and the John Forde crew clambered back into 702G-George for their next trip over the invasion beaches to assist with the big push into France.

In the attempts to encircle the German armour in the west, the 1st Canadian Army in the northern and north western Falaise sector came up against unusually fierce resistance which hampered their progress. It had been decided to help them out by getting Bomber Command to send in a few hundred bombers to add their weight to the proceedings and pitch into the enemy from above as well as the Canadians hitting them at ground level. Aiming points 21b (an armoured section) and 22 (an infantry stronghold) to the north of Falaise town were the areas that would be targeted by the Lancasters of 35 Squadron. An earlier night attack in the same area had no doubt set the scene and set defenders' nerves on edge. Subsequently the flak in the area to the south was described by the returning crews as wild and heavy. There was no doubt an understandable element of panic amongst the defenders, a lot of whom at that stage of the war were ridiculously young, inexperienced and most of them not altogether convinced of the invulnerability they had been indoctrinated with all their lives. Being bombed day and night, being pushed back on the ground and in imminent danger of being encircled was never going to be a confidence building scenario. The PFF overhead intervention in their already desperate situation was only ever going to make that a whole lot worse.

One hundred and fourteen planes were detailed for the operation that was to be led by six Mosquitos of the LNSF. The John Forde crew was again designated Master Bomber, with the 2nd Lt Hausvick crew backing them up as Deputy Master Bomber. Again it was an important operation, but yet another typical short flight time. As they had noted earlier, the Forde crew were getting used to these two to three hour afternoon jollies. A spot of lunch at midday, a short run across the channel in the afternoon and home in time for dinner. On this occasion the whole thing went very much to plan. The target area was easily identified visually and visibility remained good, certainly until the dust and smoke from the attack started to build and thicken enough to start obscuring the ground features. Several explosions were noted in the area and two huge columns of smoke were seen climbing vertically past the stream of attacking aircraft that were themselves operating close to 6,000 feet.

One senior pilot in the attack noted the Master Bomber had everything totally under control, another noted that the bombing concentration was within a 500–600 yard area and a third commented he only saw one stick of bombs outside the marked target area, though he further noted that it was actually a Halifax that was responsible. This expert witness was way back in the middle of the main bomber stream, so had ample time and opportunity to make a professional judgement on the progress of the raid. 'Something of a record for Bomber Command' was his final comment on the accuracy of the raid. Whether it was or not a record can be debated, but it was certainly a spot-on sortie and greatly assisted the Canadian ground troops in their move to close the Falaise Gap.

## Le Culot 15 August 1944

By way of a change, or several changes to be exact, the Forde crew were allotted Lancaster PB275C-Charlie for the next operation. It was to be a trip to Belgium and the opportunity to have a go at eliminating Le Culot, the ex-Luftwaffe airfield that was now home to several V1 and V2 specialist groups. Remarkably, Le Culot also known as Beauvechain, had seen only sporadic war use by the Germans and the last planes, Junkers 88s, had left just over one month earlier. As well as the airfield's Flying Bomb installations, the runways were picked out by the PFF to get the full treatment and thus prevent any further use by the Luftwaffe.

The post-raid photographs show a pattern of sixty-three direct hits in the area where the two main runways crossed. The grass areas surrounding this cruciform concrete patch were also effectively ploughed up. It is doubtful if anyone could have even walked across the airfield the next day, never mind driven a truck or tried to land a plane. The PFF were also targeting airfields at Voikel and the night fighter base at Tirlemont the same day and at much the same time.

The Forde crew in PB275 was designated the Master Bomber for this raid. Sometime before the bomb run, John Forde lost his Deputy Master Bomber whose plane suffered severe flak damage on the way to target and needed a hasty return to base to get things fixed. The Forde crew and the rest of the 35 Squadron contingent pressed on and with clear cloudless skies aiding a good visual identification and a satisfactory primary bombing pattern, the scene was set for a very successful raid. Victor's plane carried eight red TIs as well as half a dozen 1,000-lb high explosive bombs. By midday they had arrived over the target and bombed and marked for the following main bomber stream.

As expected, the post raid interrogations confirmed that it had been an accurate and successful raid with the added bonus of a direct hit on the airfield's fuel dump. Various crew reports included good concentration, accurate bombing and excellent marking. One PFF crew's report suggested that no bomb had fallen outside the airfield perimeter track.

## Stettin 16–17 August 1944

At the mouth of the River Oder, Stettin was on the Eastern edge of Germany at the time of the operation. A few years later it became Szczecin and was relocated to the western edge of Poland. Either way regardless of its name or nationality, it was that small area of Europe that was Victor's target for the night of Tuesday 16 August and it was the port complex and the associated industrial area that was the subject of the Pathfinder Force's attention.

As if to make up for some of the shorter, easier trips of recent times, this one to Stettin was one of the longest for many weeks. The crews would be airborne for the best part of eight hours with at least four or five of those flying over enemy held territory. Eight hours, initially with a heavy bomb loads, was getting towards the maximum comfortable range for the Lancaster. Just to add to the crews' discomfort, they were told that moderate to heavy flak was expected in the target area.

ND646U-Uncle was their allotted plane for this raid, and they had been allocated 2,000-lb bombs rather than the more normal 1,000-lb weaponry that they were used to on their earlier raids. For this operation they were designated Visual Centre along with four other crews from Graveley and two from 635 Squadron, with whom they were working in close company again, on this raid.

Victor's take off time was noted at 21.12½ and give or take ten minutes that was the airborne time for all the 35 Squadron planes taking part in the raid. They were over target as their watches approached 01.01. Unfortunately there was slightly more flak than they were expecting, and to add to their discomfort, they were harassed continuously by super-enthusiastic searchlight operators. Fortunately the small amount of cloud over target gave them some cover, without detracting from the bomb aimer's task of getting a good visual fix on the target area.

The bombing seemed pretty good and three or four large explosions were noted from the port area. One was noted just before the Forde crew arrived, one at about the time they were over target, with the others at times unspecified by other PFF Squadron reports. Many returning planes carried a selection of flak damage, including several having engines put out of action by the heavy flak. Surprisingly only four planes were lost overall and the subsequent photo-reconnaissance images showed that the raid had been remarkably successful, with the majority of the target area totally flattened.

Victor's crew were low on fuel on this return run and although their landing was recorded at 04.55, it was also noted that it was not at Graveley, though the exact location of the alternate landing site was not recorded in Squadron records. Whether they returned that night, or if they had a quick sleep and returned at a gentler pace the next day was not recorded either. Several other planes lost engines and others had damaged fuel lines and as such were struggling with their fuel duration. As one experienced crew record put it, 'Shaky Trip'.

## Bremen 18–19 August 1944

For the Bremen trip on the night of 18 August, Victor was once more back in the familiar turret of ND702. Designated Primary Visual Marker, they had but one main bomb, a huge 4,000-lb device guaranteed to focus the attention of people in the target area, the rest of the load being made up of their standard PFF marker pyrotechnics.

The raid was marked by Mosquitos from 608 Squadron, who also liberally Windowed the approach route and target area before commencing the target marking under the instructions of the Master Bomber. The marking was reported as tight, and the main bomber stream following in behind the Pathfinders continued with a good tight pattern of bombing. Many planes on that trip were loaded with incendiary bombs, so creating fires was obviously one of the primary raid objectives. Two very large explosions were noted by several crews during the course of the raid, one at 00.13 hours, just five or six minutes after the Forde crew let loose their 4,000-lb bomb.

In the de-briefing that followed, Victor noted that the glow from the fires from the target were still visible from 100 miles distant when 702 was heading home. It would appear from the various post raid reports, that the raid was successful on both fronts. It was time for the Roe crew to have a break from operations. Leave beckoned, and for Victor that meant Norfolk and family time.

Their regular Lancaster ND702G-George was waiting patiently on the Graveley tarmac for them when they returned a couple of weeks later. Pourchinte was to be the target that would feed them gently back into their daily routine of return trips across the channel and the bombing raids that were helping to push the Nazi forces, inch by inch, back into Germany.

## Pourchinte 31 August 1944

As the hot summer weather of 1944 drifted towards autumn, the fifteen main rocket launch sites and their supply depots along the French channel frontline were targeted for serious attention. 35 Squadron were allocated the destruction of the site at Pourchinte on 31 August.

Victor's crew were once again designated PFF Master Bomber. Unfortunately the impenetrable cloud cover convinced John Forde to keep the main bomber stream at transit height as they approached the target area, then only a few minutes later with no improvement in the situation and none likely in the immediate future he was forced to abandon the operation altogether when he realised that not even the slightest glimpse of the target was going to show through.

As they had left RAF Graveley at 06.30 that morning, they were back at base just after 09.00, still carrying their bomb loads. Fortunately there were no reports of losses from the one hundred and twenty or so aircraft that took part in the aborted sortie.

## Le Havre 5 September 1944

Victor and the Forde crew could have been forgiven for thinking they had been allocated season tickets to fly back and forth to Le Havre for the next week as they were there on five separate, frustrating occasions with every cross channel trip taken in 702G-George. However, remnants of the German army were still clinging desperately on to many scattered strongholds in the Le Havre area and although surrounded and isolated had been told by Hitler they were not to surrender and to hold to the last man.

It later appeared that it was controlled by an ex-bank manager who had hardly any military experience. He had gained his position solely because he was an ardent member of the Nazi Party. He had about 11,000 men and 115 guns available to him and but scant knowledge and little experience of what to do with them. Obviously he and his troops presented no significant hold up in the pre-ordained Allied plan, but these desperate strongholds were starting to have a high nuisance value and this was not seen as an acceptable situation within the Whitehall corridors of power.

Such anomalies had no place in an otherwise well-ordered campaign and therefore had to be removed as swiftly as possible; unsurprisingly the PFF, with support from the wider Bomber Command, were deemed to the ideal team to sort this particular problem. As well as the assistance of the RAF, they also had available several Czech artillery squads who were happy enough to keep lobbing shells into the strongholds until they were sure nothing was left breathing, standing, or otherwise showing the slightest signs of life. They would then move on to the next German stronghold, and start all over again. It was a pretty gruesome method to employ, but the Czech's hatred of the Germans was harnessed to make it an outstandingly effective way of sorting the problem.

The target areas around Le Havre were sometimes less than obvious from the air, and were given therefore a variety of code-word names for convenient identification. Wave 6, Bentley 1, and Bentley 2 were a few of the ones with memorable names and then there were the less imaginative Aiming Point 12 and The Third Aiming Point . . . all dreamed up in an office somewhere deep in the Bomber Command system.

The first of these raids for the Forde crew was on Tuesday 5 September with a take-off time of 05.06 a.m. With clear skies they had a trouble free run with a time over target of around 06.30 a.m. As a Backer-up with TIs on board they were obviously committed to two separate runs into target, one for the TIs and six minutes later the other for their bomb load. G-George bombed visually on both occasions from 13,000 feet.

The report on their bomb run concentration was good. Obviously smoke and dust and other factors played havoc with other Lancaster's runs in to target and the raid as a whole could only be rated as fair to good. However as further raids were undertaken by the PFF all that week, it was certain that no German soldier on the ground in that area was immune from an attack from the skies. This of course was in addition to the continuous attentions of the Allied ground troops and the fanatical Czech artillery teams pushing in towards them at ground level. They were not in a happy position.

## Le Havre 6 September 1944

Just a few hours later the Forde/Roe cross-channel shuttle flight was under way again, heading in much the same direction to much the same area as before, certainly with the same aim in mind. With the Murray and Mills crews from 35 Squadron taking the Master Bomber and Deputy Master Bomber roles, it fell to Victor's crew, yet again in G-George, to act as one of the Backer-up crews for this late afternoon/ early evening operation. There was just a small contingent from 35 Squadron as a larger group of the Graveley Lancasters were conducting operations against the dock area at Emden on the same day. Unfortunately Emden docks also had a large Volkswagen plant close by and a separate industrial area all located in the same vicinity and the attacking Bomber Stream seemed to share its efforts equally and only archived minimal results on each of the three targets, rather than a single concentration to obliterate one.

However, that particular problem was not one of Victor's concerns at that moment; as he and the Forde crew were due to take off an hour or so later than the 35 Squadron contingent that had been allocated to the Emden raid. Once again they were part of the operation tasked to break the Wehrmacht hold on Le Havre. They recorded a lift off time of 17.48 and headed to the east of Le Havre to take a run in to target of due west, presumably to further confuse the defenders who were almost certainly anticipating further attacks to come from the north, straight across the channel.

G-George had a load of eight TIs and six 1,000-lb ANM59 semi armour-piercing bombs. The TIs went down at 18.59 and the bombs just two and a half minutes later at 19.01.30. That must have been a fantastic piece of flying to watch ... though no doubt any observers on the ground would have had other things on their minds at the time.

To haul a part loaded Lancaster round in that short time at that speed to achieve such a tight a turn must have been working all four engines and every control surface to its absolute maximum. Fortunately by now the Ford crew were seasoned campaigners and used to sudden hard manoeuvres and the g-forces they produced, but it was certainly not a comfortable orbit, though it obviously got the job done, and done well.

There were no reports of fighters or flak at the target area, and none on the flights in to or away from target. The post-raid report for G-George gave their bombing accuracy as good, but Victor saw the nearby railway line get hit as well as the target specified. At 20.09 they landed back at base went through the de-brief and no doubt headed for a well-earned pint in the mess.

## Le Havre 8 September 1944

Victor, John Forde and the rest of the crew of G-George had a day off on 7 September, though almost certainly the defending German troops at the Le Havre garrison didn't. By the early morning of Friday 8 September, ND702 was scheduled and prepared for another return trip to Le Havre. For this sortie, 35 Squadron provided the Master Bomber, Deputy Master Bomber and four Backer-up crews.

Unfortunately the gods of the weather conspired against them, or more to the point, in favour of the defenders, and the cloud base descended to a little over 2,000 feet. By that point, at 07.35 p.m. the Master Bomber F/O Murray called off the attack with just a few bombs being dropped as a trial run to see just what was possible. The answer was nothing. There was only a single flak gun operating in the area, so defences were light.

A later PFF raid the same day arrived in the target overhead sometime around 18.30 that evening and had similar luck with the weather. They too tried a few bomb runs, 'just to see how it went' and then had to call the raid off and come home disappointed. They would all have to go again.

## Le Havre 9 September 1944

As it transpired the same crews in the same planes planned the same route the next day, and sad to say achieved the same result. 10/10 cloud down to 2,000 feet on the Saturday still prevented them pressing home the attack and prompted one post-raid report to state, 'Attack impossible.' (At least that was the sanitised version logged into the system for official consumption).

Fortunately all six of 35 Squadron's Lancasters made it back. All the crews had understood that the operation had to be repeated, but to repeat it and still have the same negative result due to low cloud was particularly galling. They would simply have to continue repeating the operation until it was a success. They crossed their fingers for better luck the next day.

## Le Havre 10 September 1944

The next return trip to Le Havre would be their last ever flight in Lancaster ND702. Unsurprisingly it was also the day Bomber Command started to get really upset with the weather and lack of progress at Le Havre, so a total of eight PFF-led raids, containing 992 planes were planned for that day, all tasked with sorting the Le Havre situation once and for all. Two raids included Lancasters from 35 Squadron. 'Alvis 1' was the target area for the other Graveley attack and Bentley 1 and Bentley 2 were undertaken at the same time by 635 squadron from Downham Market.

Victor and the Forde crew were on the six-ship PFF formation from Graveley on the second Le Havre raid. They were airborne at about 3.15 p.m. Looking at other take-off times and the extra mileage the different squadrons needed to cover to get to target, it looks as if Bomber Command had it in mind that these raids could provide the, 'all hell that broke loose' in eight separate places, all at the same time.

For once, the Met Flight forecast was clear over target, and yet again that week the Met Flight boys were spot on. Now it was time to play catch-up. The Master Bomber reported that the target area was identified before they had even crossed the English coast, and that the strong winds on the ground in the area were clearing the smoke and dust so well that the target was visible almost all the time. This was much more like it.

The enthusiasm of Bomber Command to put on a giant *tour de force* in such a small area, created the unusual effect of one squadron's planes attacking another squadron's designated targets. Some would argue that was no big deal provided they hit the required spot. It is not confirmed in the reports anywhere that any of the squadron commanders involved saw it in quite the same light.

The Ford Crew were designated Master Bomber for this operation and had Squadron Leader Bromley backing them as their Deputy Master Bomber. With a civilised take off time just after 15.15 allocated, they were able to run in to target at 16.20 and drop their marker TIs. They bombed from 6,400 feet, but for some reason the main bomber stream bombing patterns became erratic. That, however, did not stop two major explosions being reported, one at 16.32 and the other at 16.33. They arrived back at Graveley at 17.41. That was their last trip to Le Havre and their last trip in 702.

A further visit by other members of 35 Squadron was planned for 11 September and the target areas code-named Cadillac 1 and Cadillac 2 would see the finishing touches to the Le Havre air campaign. It had been a long week for Victor and the Forde crew, with less to show for their efforts than they would have liked. The French coast would still however command their full attention for the next two days as they were off next to pay a visit to the port of Calais. Then it would be time for leave, a rest and a re-charging of the crew's personal batteries. It was also time to mark the arrival of Pilot John Forde's first child, an opportunity for a pint or two not to be missed by any right thinking airman.

After completing twenty-three operations with John Forde at the front and Victor guarding the rear, ND702 was then handed over to the Bradburn crew, and the Forde Crew headed off on leave. It was one of those ironic twists of fate that happen in wartime, on the very next trip ND702G-George was posted in the squadron records as, 'Failed to return'. Five of the Bradburn crewmembers were reported as KIA, the remaining two as POWs.

## Calais 27 September 1944

Again a small concentrated area of French countryside, this time around Calais was bequeathed some pretty unimaginative target references, with just Aiming Point and numbers (i.e. Aiming Point 20) being the best Bomber Command could come up with. Some fifty Mosquitos from the LNSF were to lead the way with almost 500 PFF led heavy bombers from Bomber Command. Unsurprisingly many targets were to be hit simultaneously. Before the operation that Wednesday morning, several other raids on the 24, 25 and 26 September had all targeted the area around Calais; it looked very much as if it was going to be re-run of Le Havre.

On their return from leave, as 'their' Lancaster 702 was no longer available, Victor's crew had been allocated ND907G-George and the role of Master Bomber for this operation. Squadron Leader Green joined the Forde crew as 2nd Bomb Aimer. Squadron Leader Bromley would again be their Deputy Master Bomber in PB566. Again all involved agreed it was a rather civilised hour to start a combat operation, with Victor's Lancaster getting airborne at a 9.45 a.m. in the morning and the rest of the small 35 Squadron contingent following soon after. They arrived over target at. 10.39.10 and immediately ran in, dropping their TIs.

Their bomb run was timed at 10.46.30. Despite corrective action by John Forde, the bombing pattern became more scattered and he decided that that it was time to abandon the raid and head for home. G-George landed 11.53 just in time for lunch.

## Calais 28 September 1944

Even after all the previous operations, there was still more progress to be made in the Calais area, so a further set of raids were organised for Thursday 28 September. Victor's crew were again allocated the role of Master Bomber on the early morning cross channel run. There was a very small but select team from 35 Squadron. Just three planes were allotted to the raid; the Forde crew as Master Bomber, Squadron Leader Bromley as the Deputy Master Bomber in PB566 and F/O Moreden in PB343 as a Backer-up.

Some fifty Mosquitos from LNSF led the way and close to 500 of Bomber Command's finest followed just a few minutes behind. Cloud was estimated at five tenths, but still with good visibility. The good news from this attack was that there were no flak batteries left operational in the area. The Luftwaffe was unable to mount any fighter cover and subsequently there were no Allied casualties incurred in the raid.

The downside to this were the reports indicating that the bombing was scattered with serious undershoot patterns, such that John Forde deemed it necessary to call off this second consecutive raid as it was not achieving its aims. Victor's timetable for this raid had been:

Take off at 09.45 a.m.
Time over target (TIs) 10.39.10 a.m.
Time over target (bombs) 10.46.30 a.m.
Return to base 11.53 a.m.

Another frustrating day for 35 Squadron.

Fortunately their next operational sortie was several days away, as Victor's promotion to Warrant Officer (acting) arrived after the Calais raids, so a spot of serious celebrating was in order before they headed off back to Europe.

## Saarbrücken 5 October 1944

The Forde crew were getting quietly annoyed with the way the weather was contriving to spoil their operations. They all hoped that their next raid, this time into Germany, to the railway marshalling yards at Saarbrücken, would bring a change in fortune and provide them with a fully completed, totally successful, operation. They were tasked to destroy these particular yards as they were being used to help move forward thousands of German infantry reserves who were desperately needed by the Wehrmacht to block the American push in towards Saarbrücken itself.

Unfortunately there was to be no change of fortune for Victor's crew. They were again in 907G-George, and allocated the role of Primary Marker. Again, much to their annoyance, the cloud cover was one hundred per cent and as such that the target area was never visible. As it turned out, the TIs that were dropped on the H2S radar information only served to confuse matters further as the cloud produced a distracting pattern of light that was never going to be distinct enough to target any bombs.

In the post raid de-brief John Forde held an opinion that probably too many TIs had been dropped and that had contributed to the indistinct foggy glare that hampered the target identification. Other 35 Squadron crew reports indicated that bombs from the main bomber force had been seen to fall anything between four and ten miles off target. Not a good day.

## Fort Fredrick Hendrik 11 October 1944

Victor was once again in the rear turret of ND907G-George for an attack on the Fort Fredrik Hendrik gun batteries on the southern bank of the river Scheldt in Holland, on Wednesday 11 October. The earlier forecast from Met Flight was positive and gave a clear sky that morning with no cloud over the target area. The Forde crew breathed a collective sigh of relief. However it turned out to be an over-optimistic call and the raid could not be completed.

By the late afternoon when the second of the three waves, including 907, arrived over the River Scheldt, there was a full 10/10 cloud cover over target. Again they were forced to abandon the mission.

It was the first time the Forde crew had flown with a Long Stop Master Bomber at their disposal, even though they in this case could not utilise him. Surprisingly a couple of planes had an unexpected opportunity to make a spontaneous attack when a small gap in the cloud, immediately over the target area, coincided with their arrival. Several good hits, however lucky, were gratefully noted as a small reward for a great deal of effort from a number of crews.

Victor was no doubt delighted to hear that the third raid of the series on Fort Fredrik, early the next morning was blessed with clearer skies and a decent view of the target, thus at last managing to achieve the required results.

## Duisburg 14–15 October 1944

Prior to this operation, all the aircrews of Bomber Command had been stood down and rested for the previous forty-eight hours. Thus when their C-in-C Sir Arthur Harris had been requested to provide an overwhelming show of strength, and combine with the USAAF as a clear demonstration of might to the Nazi authorities, he was able to muster some 1,013 planes. This was to undertake a daylight raid on the morning of Saturday 14 October. It would be integrated with a raid by the Americans and a further night raid would follow in the early hours of the Sunday morning. This show of strength was intended to reinforce the idea that further military resistance was only ever going to end in failure. As we now know, the German High Command was too wrapped up with its own delusions and wild propaganda to understand the truth when it was staring them in the face. Victor's war would therefore continue unabated.

And continue it did with the PFF-led overnight raid to Duisburg, again in ND907G-George. F/O Blackband had brought it back from the daylight raid that morning and handed it back to its ground crew, who now had just about ten hours to service it, fix and snags, get it re-loaded and ready for John Forde to take it on its next trip to Duisburg. The turnaround time achieved by the ground crews was exceptional. By using most planes for a second time that day, a sixteen-ship group left Graveley just after 23.15 that evening. G-George was loaded with four 1,000-lb ANM59s, one 4,000-lb HC and eight green TIs, of which four were standard and four were the long burn versions.

The Forde crew noted in their post-raid report that the defences they had been briefed to expect seemed to be caught by surprise, almost certainly by being on the receiving end of three substantial raids in less than twenty-four hours. An alternative view could be that the first two raids had given them such a battering, that the limited defences that Victor experienced were the best efforts the defence force could muster at the time. Either way it allowed for an extremely successful raid with good marking and concentrated, effective bombing. Fires from the previous raids were still burning well when they ran in onto the target and the additional fires they started with their sortie, were still visible to Victor as they coasted out on the way home. By 03.15 that morning Victor was back at base and headed to the de-brief with all the other the Graveley crews who had returned around that same time, without incident. It started to make up a little for all the frustrating disappointments of the Le Havre and Calais operations.

Sadly this was to be the last sortie for the Forde crew as a unit, as they had reached the end of their tour. Having been a real 'band of brothers' for so long, it was now time for career choices to be made and for each to go their own separate ways. John Forde, Don Caruthers and John Rollins elected to move on to Transport Command and retrain on the Douglas DC3. They had opted for a slightly less adventurous life in the Far East, moving freight and personnel, although it has to be remembered that no military aviation in those days was without its moments.

Victor on the other hand was still very much up for the fight and requested another tour with the Pathfinders. It was understandably not a problem for the RAF and with his continuance as aircrew agreed he was granted his option of staying with 35 Squadron.

He was allocated to the Watson crew who were no doubt more than delighted to get such an experienced set of eyes and trigger fingers for their new Tail End Charlie. It seems again that the PFF had got it right and everyone was happy. There appears to be no surviving record of the farewell moments of the Forde crew as they went their separate ways, but like most wartime posting situations, it was probably just a swift pint at the pub and all over in moments.

# 7

# Operations—November– December 1944

By now the Allied push into Europe was making good, solid, if unspectacular, progress inland and the Red Army was inexorably pushing the dispirited Wehrmacht back towards the German heartland on a daily, if not hourly, basis. The final outcome to the war was obvious; the only discussion point was the exact timing. As one commentator of the day noted, 'The writing was on the wall, but no one in the Reichstag was reading it.'

Back at Graveley, despite the total change of crew, Victor was rather pleased to find himself still in his favourite seat at the back end of Lancaster ND907G-George. However there was now a whole new team around him, his life had moved on. His new crew were,

| | |
|---|---|
| F/L F. Watson | Pilot |
| P/O Ken Smith | Navigator |
| F/O S. Scott | Bomb Aimer |
| W/O Les Holland | Mid-Upper Gunner |
| Sgt. R. Grayson | Wireless Operator |
| W/O Victor Roe | Rear Gunner |
| Sgt. G. Cross | Engineer |

(Sgt Grayson was later replaced by F/Sgt, J. H. Hacker, who was in turn replaced by F/O F. J. Pentelow of the Royal New Zealand Air Force.)

## Düsseldorf 2 November 1944

The Watson crew already had some combat experience and so were immediately deemed available for operations and designated as a PFF Supporter for this sortie. ND907 was loaded for the trip with the PFF standard of one 4,000-lb bomb, five 1,000-lb bombs and six 500-lb bombs. With no cloud and good visibility to help them, the new crew got off to a great start and completed a highly successful first operation together.

It was three of the main industrial areas of Düsseldorf, Düsseltal, Derendorf and Stockum that were selected for the raid and some 992 aircraft from Bomber Command made the trip that Thursday. Rather surprisingly only six were needed from 35 Squadron. Thirty-one LNSF Mosquitos led the raid with the usual liberal dropping of Window to confuse the German radar defences. Those same Mosquitos then continued on to target to be the first marker planes there and to be the first to drop their bomb loads, which for them by this time in the war was usually a single 4,000-lb high explosive 'Cookie'. The raid on Düsseldorf turned out to be an exceptionally accurate one that was, assisted greatly by good visibility and a distinct lack of cloud, which in turn permitted the PFF crews to actually see their targets for once. Unfortunately the weather situation also aided the defenders in much the same way and the increased visibility enabled the Ack-Ack crews to claim an alarming nineteen RAF planes brought down. Take off for the Watson crew had been at ten minutes to five and their return touchdown time logged in at just before 21.15.

## Bochum 4–5 November 1944

The demolition of the Bochumer Verein steel plant in Bochum was the operation planned for the weekend November 4–5 1944. It was another of Bomber Command's major raids and a massive fleet of planes numbering just short of seven hundred and fifty was earmarked for the job. Also allocated for the trip that day were some 10,000 high explosive bombs and 130,000 incendiary devices. No one at Bomber Command or PFF Squadron Level was going to accept anything but total success; that was blindingly obvious.

PB288R-Robert was the plane allocated to the Victor and the Watson crew, who had again been designated as a PFF Supporter for this raid. They had a 'standard' Supporter bomb load of one 4000-lb HG bomb, two 1,000-lb AMN65 bombs, and six 500-lb GP and four 1,000-lb MC bombs.

Bochum was another industrial complex in the Ruhr valley, midway between Dortmund and Essen, both places Victor had visited earlier in his Pathfinder career. The Bochumer steel works was one of the most essential industrial plants for the Nazi continuance of the war. If this raid could bomb it out of existence, it would represent a large, long-term blow to the continuing production of weapons and munitions for the German military. As it was to unfold that night, the plant would indeed be damaged beyond repair by the end of the raid and would take no further part in the war. But that outcome was still a few hours away. Victor and his new crew had yet to pay the Bochum works a visit, only after that would its production figures drop to zero.

They were in the first wave of the attack on this operation and so took off from Graveley at 16.50 and headed back to the familiar territory of the Ruhr Valley. Once more they had good visibility and clear skies to aid their progress and arrived in the target overhead after roughly two and a half hours in the air at 19.12.48. The target was clearly visual, accurately marked and cross referenced to the H2S system. The aircraft doing the marking had however obviously attracted the attention of the nearby Ack-Ack gun battery. They and their opposite numbers manning the searchlights, both did their level best to make life impossible for the incoming attackers.

There were however no enemy fighters to be seen by 35 Squadron in their Pathfinder role, although Bomber Command's losses were very heavy that night due to the intensity of the flak and an attack by Ju88 night fighters on the main bomber stream. The loss rate so angered C-in-C Bomber Command, Sir Arthur Harris that he ordered an enquiry into the planning and conduct of the raid to establish why so many crews had been lost.

The bombing from 17,500 feet for the Watson crew achieved a good bomb pattern and equally good results. Two particularly large explosions were noted at 19.28, then again just two minutes later at 19.30. One report gave the estimated flame height of the first explosion in excess of 1,000 feet. Surviving records appear to show that the factory had over 10,000 HE and 130,000 incendiary bombs in store when it was hit.

As with previously successful raids in the same area, Victor only lost sight of the fires that had been started by the attack, once they had been nearly an hour into their return journey home. For the second time running the new team flew back to base feeling pretty good about their day's work. They landed back at RAF Graveley at exactly 21.13 ½. 35 Squadron's fraction-conscious intelligence officer was obviously back on duty.

## Gelsenkirchen 6 November 1944

The target in the Gelsenkirchen area was the synthetic oil plant at Nordstern, which appears to be recorded under both town names in various PFF Squadron reports. ND916 now re-designated K-King, was the allotted plane for Victor's next trip. It had been some five months since he last had last flown in 916, which like him had no doubt logged thousands of rather precarious combat miles in the interim, and was probably by now starting to show signs of wear. The forecast for the day included 10/10ths cloud cover at 10,000 feet and the Met Flight were once again spot on.

As the attack height was set at the PFF standard 18,000 feet most crews found the markers difficult to spot, so the majority of Lancasters dropped on H2S, or the positioning of previous bomb blasts. One report from another squadron saw a glimpse of the target through a break in the clouds and caught sight of one of the giant cooling towers at the plant take a direct hit, so it was assumed that the H2S system was working fine that day. The Master Bomber had then felt confident enough to also mark the second target, the town of Gelsenkirchen itself. This had the double effect of taking out both the housing and infrastructure to support the workers at the plant, thus achieving a devastating blow to the oil production.

35 Squadron put up thirteen Lancasters for this raid, including the Master Bomber and Deputy Master Bomber, as well as planes in a variety of other PFF support roles. All 35 Squadron participants appeared to have a successful trip and all returned to Graveley without any reported problems. The flak was classed as only moderate and again no one saw any sign of any Luftwaffe fighters.

The rumours in the mess were that the lack of fighter opposition was possibly due to petrol supplies becoming scarce as a result of the success of the raids such as this one on the Nordstern plant. Whether it was true or not did not matter to Victor, he was delighted that it appeared to have worked and the defensive fighter cover was diminishing.

## Freiburg 27 November 1944

After a few weeks away, another familiar plane from Victor's past, PB257T-Tommy, was again allocated to his crew for the longer run to the city of Freiburg on the edge of the Black Forest in southern Germany. They were assigned the job of PFF Blind Illuminator for the raid. It would be a full five-and-a-half-hour trip from lift off to touch down, a sharp reminder to Victor that the runs across the channel to France in the late summer really had been a bit of a soft touch.

35 Squadron contributed twelve Lancasters to this operation, which, despite a 7/10 cloud cover, proved to be another very successful raid. They bombed from 14,000 feet using a combination of their own H2S and the visible TIs. The Master Bomber made the decision to mark the secondary target half way through the raid, as the results he was seeing appeared to indicate that the primary target was pretty much destroyed. The local railway tracks nearby also got their share of punishment, which added to the feeling of the returning crews that it had really been a job well done. It was also interesting to note that of the twelve planes from 35 Squadron, three contained Wing Commanders; W/Cdrs Coulson, Cracknell and Bromley. It is also worth noting there were four 35 Squadron Lancasters on the attack on the industrial complex at Neuss that was taking place the same day, and at the same time. 35 Squadron were being kept busy.

The next day one of Victor's favourite planes, the much travelled Lancaster ND907 was taxied off its 35 Squadron hardstand for the last time and flown by a ferry pilot to the Pathfinder Training Unit just down the road at RAF Warboys, where it was put to work for the rest of its active life, training new Pathfinder crews.

## Dortmund 29 November 1944

ME355O-Oboe was the new plane allocated to Victor's crew for the raid on Dortmund itself. ME355 had been delivered just two weeks earlier on 15 November from No. 32 Maintenance Unit at RAF St Athan in South Wales. Compared to many of the other planes that Victor had been allocated in the past, this one was so little used that it still actually smelled new.

It was Victor's second trip to Dortmund, the first being almost six months earlier. The Watson crew were Blind Secondary Markers for this trip and had a mixture of bombs ranging from one at 4,000 lb, five at 1,000 lb and six at 500 lb. They bombed from 18,000 feet through cloud and ground haze via their H2S system, and although there were few visual reports of damage inflicted, the Watson crew felt they had met with some measure of success. They returned to base at just after five o'clock that afternoon, to be met with the sad news that the Thorpe crew in PB199 was missing. Suddenly 35 Squadron felt that their run of good fortune was over.

## Heimbach 4 December 1944

An Oboe-equipped Mosquito from the LNSF led the PFF heavy contingent and the following main bomber stream on the raid that Monday. The aim was to wreak havoc with the dam feeding the Heimbach hydro-electric plant, which contributed essential electrical power to the Rhineland area of west Germany near the Eifel Mountains.

Again the Watson crew were allocated the role of Supporter and had the usual array of ordnance loaded for the trip. When they arrived in the overhead at 17,000 feet, the target was visible as well as marked with red TIs, so a good bombing concentration was observed.

It was a straight five-hour sortie with take-off recorded at 18.51 and landing listed at 23.51. Of the planes from 35 Squadron, only the Leicester crew had problems, and they lost some control authority over the aileron system on PB578F-Fox during their climb to cruise altitude and were forced to abort.

By the time they landed back at Graveley Victor's crew were, all pretty tired. They felt it had been another long day, not only for them but for all of the crews from 35 Squadron. However that was far from the end of the matter for Victor and the Watson crew, the planning team at Graveley allocated them three more sorties to follow without a break. It was a busy time.

## Soest 5 December 1944

The town of Soest in North Rhine/Westphalia was home to some of the largest railway marshalling yards in Germany and the strategically important Akku Hagen battery works that made accumulators for the German U-Boat fleet. Other industrial plants in the close proximity were engaged in war work making tank tracks and other vital military vehicle components. It was a strange situation where inaccurate bombing in an area with such closely situated targets would probably still be successful. The marshalling yards were distinctly visible running almost southeast to northwest across the northern town boundary. The raid was as usual led by an LNSF Oboe Mosquito and they ran in at 177 degrees, thus aligning the bomb run with the railway features.

A few reports gave some of the Lancaster's bomb loads undershooting by almost a mile, but on the track they were flying to get to the target area they probably damaged large swathes of the railway structure anyway. Several fires were seen in the area and one very large explosion was noted at 21.10, just as the majority of the planes were running in on target.

## Mersberg 6 December 1944

Mersberg was reported to be the most heavily defended area in mainland Europe at the time of the raid, with a protective ring of some 400 flak batteries, more than twice the number of anti-aircraft guns that protected Berlin. Sprawling over three-square miles of German real estate and dotted with over two hundred buildings and dozens of decoy buildings, the Mersberg synthetic oil plant was crucial to the Nazi war machine. Officially named the IG Interessengemeinschaft Farbenindustrie AG Luna Works, was frequently reduced by the Allied High Command to just the Luna Works for ease of conversation. As you can imagine, this happened often during the Second World War, as the RAF attacked it twice and the USAAF 8th Air Force, no less than twenty times.

The plant was a great place to avoid if you lived in the area. Almost 6,552 bombers delivered 18,328 tons of high explosives on the plant and kept busy the nineteen thousand employees who also manned the Ack-Ack guns liberally distributed around the huge site. It had the unenviable record of being one of the most regularly bombed areas of Germany.

It was a six-hour round trip for Victor's Lancaster O-Oboe from Graveley to Mersberg and back; a taxing enough raid due to distance alone. Then they had to tackle the main transit phase of a couple of hours over some of the most heavily defended parts of the German heartland. When that was over it was immediately followed by the run in to target on one of the most fortified industrial sites the enemy had.

You can imagine the prospect of that certainly gave Victor and his crew a few things to think about as they throttled up the four Merlins and lead the 35 Squadron contingent off down Graveley's runway, late that afternoon. It was almost 17.20 when they lifted off, but it was well past half-past eight by the time the target area approached beneath them, once more they were confronted by a target protected by a total cloud undercast. Undeterred they bombed on their H2S readings and turned for home confident it had been a reasonably successful raid with generally a good pattern of marking and some reasonably tight bombing. However one sky marker appeared a couple of miles off and at least one bomber unloaded their bomb load using it.

A very large explosion in the target area was noted by other crews in the main bomber stream a few minutes before nine o'clock, just as most of the Graveley contingent was concentrating on getting clear of the area and heading for home. Flak in the area was noted as heavy in many of the reports and others commented that a reasonable show was put up by the defenders on the way home. All the crews from 35 Squadron got home safely. O-Oboe landed back just after midnight.

## Ludwigshafen 15–16 December 1944

The chemical works of IG Farbenindustrie AG works at Ludwigshafen was next on the list of industrial targets for the Pathfinder Force. It was another important synthetic oil plant in Ludwigshafen itself, and was close to the Ludwigshafen railway marshalling yards. The main industrial estate was only a couple of miles from the Oppau plant. It was an area of very rich pickings for all bomber crews, and the planners really were spoilt for choice. As with the Mersberg plant, the RAF and the USAAF made repeated raids on the complex during the latter stages of the war, and naturally the Germans plant operators made strenuous efforts to maintain, repair or rebuild what was left after each raid. It was a non-ending game of 'tit for tat'.

Once more with 335 as their trusted Lancaster, the Watson crew carried their standard PFF Supporter bomb load of one 4,000-lb bomb, six 1,000-lb bombs and two 500-lb bombs. Again they had a long run to target with a great deal of heavy flak to deal with on the way, but this time the flak actually eased in the target area. This they took as an indication that there were probably night fighters in the area. Fortunately there were none seen.

As there were no searchlights observed in the area either, for the Graveley crews from that point of view, it was a copybook operation. They also had clear visibility and only a small amount of industrial haze, which made marking and bombing much easier and the results of both were seen to be very good. They bombed from 18,000 feet. Large fires were seen to start and propagate in the area and Victor got his usual grandstand view of all this as they started the long haul home. Other squadron reports on the raid rated it 'one of the best ever seen' and confirming Victor's thoughts on the fires started, another report claimed that the smoke was at 10,000 feet and still climbing by the time the last Lancasters were departing.

All Graveley crews returned safely, but the Poley crew had been forced back early with one of the starboard engines out of action. They made some bombs safe to

1 Almost a year after the loss of the Watson crew, Victor's sister Kate and brother-in-law Ernest Foyster go to Buckingham Palace to receive Victors Medals. Kate seen wearing the DFM and the CGM.

2 The annual photo for Mr Fegan's Home for Boys at Stony Stratford. Year 1935. Victor Roe is in the 5th row, 2nd from left.

3 The official RAF photo. Sgt. Victor Roe. DFM, CGM.

4 Victor's early days at Mr Fegan's home for boys at Stoney in Stratford.

5 Victor, sometime between leaving Mr Fegan's and joining the RAF.

6 Victor peering out of the rear turret of 'his' Handley-Page Halifax.

7 Victor about to become RAF Aircrew. The last few days as a civilian.

8 Victor with the members of his first crew. (The J. [Jack] Forde crew).

9 Victor and his second crew. (The F. Watson crew)

10 Victor front left with the Forde crew in front of Lancaster ND755 used only once by them on the night of 22–23 May for the raid on Dortmund.

11 The Forde crew dressed for work.

12 The Watson crew also kitted up ready to head out to Germany.

13 The Forde crew having the luxury of a second crew photo.

14 The workhorse of RAF Bomber Command, the Avro Lancaster.

15 One of the Wellingtons that Victor flew in the few weeks between 22 and 31 August before moving on to the four-engine Halifax.

16 Victor's Handley Page Halifax on a low level training sortie, early in the flying career of the John Forde crew.

17 An Avro Lancaster from 35 Squadron, Graveley, high above the clouds. A common sight over wartime England, and an increasingly common sight over occupied Europe and Germany, after D-Day as the allies started the long push to Berlin.

18 Aerial shot of Dresden taken after the war's end.

19 Victor's favourite plane, the Avro Lancaster. This is one of the twenty-four different examples of the Lancaster he flew as a member of the Pathfinder Force.

20 Victor Roe earning his DFM. The Bf110 has disabled this rear turret, and the pilot, John Forde is yawing the plane at Victor's instructions, to give him the field of fire he needs inflict terminal damage on the attacker.

21 The Forde crew heading off to mainland Europe, as part of the Pathfinder Force.

22. Ground crew load the Lancasters for their next trip into Europe. (Joe Bamford)

23 The Halifax was Victor and the Forde crew's first experience of a heavy bomber, and lasted over the winter of 1943, from late December 1943 until early March 1944.

24 Pathfinder Lancasters from 35 Squadron crossing into enemy held territory.

| YEAR 1943 | | AIRCRAFT | | PILOT, OR 1ST PILOT | 2ND PILOT, PUPIL OR PASSENGER | DUTY (INCLUDING RESULTS AND REMARKS) |
|---|---|---|---|---|---|---|
| MONTH | DATE | Type | No. | | | |
| | | | | | | TOTALS BROUGHT FORWARD |
| JULY | 15 | XL. W. | XL.W. | SELF | CREW. HOUGHTON. | FORMATION. 50mins. |
| " | 16 | XL. P. | XL.P. | SELF | CREW. | LOOKIE. |
| " | 17 | XL. Z. | XL.Z. | F/O. FOX. | SELF, | CHECK CONVERSION. |
| " | 18 | XL. V. | XL.V. | SELF | CREW. | LNE BOMBING. |
| " | 18 | WELLINGTON. | XL.V. | SELF | CREW. JONES. | CROSS COUNTRY. |
| " | 21 | WELLINGTON | XL.P. | SELF | CREW. | FORMATION. 45 mins. |
| " | 22 | WELLINGTON | XL.Z. | SELF. | CREW. GLYNE. | CIRCUIT. A/C. U/S. |
| " | 24 | WELLINGTON | XL.Z. | SELF | | FERRY. |
| " | 24 | WELLINGTON | XL.Z. | SELF | CREW. | FORMATION. 1.30 |
| " | 24 | WELLINGTON | XL.P. | SELF | CREW. GOODING. | CROSS COUNTRY. FORMATION. .30 |
| " | 25 | WELLINGTON | XL.V. | SELF | CREW. | CROSS COUNTRY. |
| " | 26 | WELLINGTON | XL.V. | SELF | CREW GOODING. | CROSS COUNTRY. |
| " | 22 | WELLINGTON | XL.M. | F/O ROBINSON | SELF. ROE. | FIGHTER AFFILIATION. |

TOTALS OPERATIONAL TRAINING FLIGHT.

O.C. J. FLIGHT ........ S/LR.

O.C. TRAINING WING. ........ W/OR.

GRAND TOTAL [Cols. (1) to (10)] 384 Hrs. 35 Mins.

TOTALS CARRIED FORWARD

25 Pilot's logbook Wellington OTU. Victor's training records (Fighter Affiliation exercise on 22 July 22 1943).

By 466 (R.A.A.F.) SQUADRON.   SECRET   PAGE No. 217

FOR THE MONTH OF AUGUST, 19 43.

| DATE | AIRCRAFT Type & Number | CREW | DUTY | Time Up | Time Down | DETAILS OF SORTIE OR FLIGHT | REFERENCES. |
|---|---|---|---|---|---|---|---|
| 30/31.8.43 | WELLINGTON X HE-351 | Aus.416802 P/O.Stevens J.H. | Captain | 00.30 | 05.33 | Primary attacked from 18,000 feet at 02.47 hours. | |
| | | Sgt.Collins S. | B/A. | | | No T.I. could be definitely identified so aircraft | |
| | | Aus.410478 P/O.Fryer R.H.S. | Nav. | | | bombed large fire near which T.I.s were seen | |
| | | Sgt.Green D.D.G. | W/A.G. | | | falling on approach to target. Two large patches | |
| | | Aus.426005 F/S.Harris L.F. | A/G. | | | of fire and many small scattered fires. Monica | |
| | | | | | | fitted. 4-5/10 Strato-cu. cloud at 10,000 feet. | |
| | WELLINGTON X HE-989 | Aus.403904 P/O.Cairns J.D. | Captain | 00.12 | 04.59 | Primary attacked from 18,500 feet at 02.30 hours. | |
| | | Sgt.Wiffen W.N. | B/A. | | | Identified by one Red and 3 Green T.I.s. Bombed | |
| | | Aus.414847 F/S.Shine P. | Nav. | | | with Red in sight seen to cascade at 02.28. Numerous | |
| | | Aus.414319 F/S.Rigby C. | W/A.G. | | | small fires seen in target area. Monica carried | |
| | | Aus.414159 F/S.Oliver A.C.H. | A/G. | | | and serviceable. 7/10 at 9000 feet, over target. | |
| | WELLINGTON X LN-442 | P/O.Forde J.A. | Captain | 00.11 | 05.14 | Primary attacked from 18,000 feet at 02.14 hours. | |
| | | P/O.Werner H.K. | B/A. | | | Identified by P.F.F. Red and Green T.I.s. Bombed | |
| | | P/O.Rollins J.H. | Nav. | | | with single Red in sight, seen to cascade at 02.11. | |
| | | Sgt.Cerruthers D. | W/A.G. | | | Reds and Greens plentiful prior to bombing. | |
| | | Sgt.Roe V.A. | A/G. | | | Numerous small scattered fires seen, covering whole | |
| | | | | | | target area. Monica fitted and serviceable. | |
| | | | | | | 4-5/10ths Cloud - tops approx. 8,000 feet, very | |
| | | | | | | good visibility. | |
| 31.8.43/ 1.9.43. | | | | | | SPECIAL TARGET - BOMBING ATTACK. | A17 |
| | | | | | | Summary. | 889 |
| | | | | | | Twelve aircraft were ordered and took off and | 76 |
| | | | | | | eleven made a highly successful attack on the target, | |
| | | | | | | the twelfth aircraft did not bomb owing to a bomb | |
| | | | | | | sight failure. All aircraft carried 8 - 500 lb. | |
| | | | | | | G.P. bombs. | |
| | | | | | | There appears to have been a small amount of broken | |

26 Squadron records, the entry for one of Victor's five operations with the Wellington.

| Date | Aircraft Type & Number | Crew | Duty | Time Up | Time Down | Details of Sortie or Flight | References |
|---|---|---|---|---|---|---|---|
| 29/30.12.43 | HALIFAX III HX-266 | Aus.413239 P/O.McDonald S.R. Aus.410202 F/S.Evans R.J. Aus.412562 F/S.Maunder J.H. Aus.410686 F/S.Mitchell G.J. Aus.426402 F/S.Tranent K.M. Aus.426622 F/S.Rourke P.J. Sgt.Greenwood R. | Captain B/A. Nav. W/AG. R/G MU/AG. F/E. | 17.16 | 18.48 | No attack made. Inter-comm. failure, and unable to rectify this, so Captain decided to return. Bombs were jettisoned 'Safe' at 17.55 hours from 9,000 feet at 54.40N. 01.23E. | |
| | HALIFAX III HX-267 | Aus.6104 P/O.Curnow L.D. Aus.415197 F/S.Trewern W.C. Aus.420411 P/O.Wade J.E. Sgt.Garbutt R.H. Sgt.Forrester W. Aus.424611 Sgt.Williamson L.G. Sgt.Stellard T.E. | Captain B/A. Nav. W/AG. R/G. MU/AG. F/E. | 17.27 | 23.39 | Primary attacked from 22,000 feet at 20.12 hours. 036°M. Bombed on centre of fire red/green flares which cascaded about 2010 hours. 10/10 Cloud. | |
| | HALIFAX III HX-271 | Aus.413604 F/S.Johnson A.L. Aus.417406 Sgt.Paice N.D. Aus.410273 F/S.Williams J.S. Aus.416309 F/S.Liddle J.E.L. Aus.422515 F/S.Harrop R.E. Aus.403460 F/O.Penman E.L. Sgt.Silburn J. | Captain B/A. Nav. W/AG. R/G. MU/AG. F/E. | 17.15 | 23.51 | Primary attacked from 19,000 feet at 20.15 hours. 035°M. Bombed on centre of 3 Red/Green flares cascaded. 10/10 St.cu. cloud. | |
| | HALIFAX III HX-274 | Aus.416602 P/O.Stevens J.H. Aus.16480 F/S.Dawson H. Aus.410478 F/O.Fryor R.H. P/O.Green D.D. Sgt.Roe V.A. Aus.417351 F/S.Kemp L.A. Sgt.Rimmer O.A. | Captain B/A. Nav. W/AG. R/G. MU/AG. F/E. | 17.20 | 00.17 | Primary attacked from 22,000 feet at 20.18 hours. 035°M. Bombed centre of line of eight flares. 10/10 Cloud at about 12,000 feet, slight haze from operations height to cloud below. | |

27 Squadron records, Victor's Halifax posting, again just one of five combat operational operations.

| | | | | | | Time carried forward :- | 87.10 | 64·05 |
|---|---|---|---|---|---|---|---|---|
| Date | Hour | Aircraft Type and No. | Pilot | Duty | | Remarks (including results of bombing, gunnery, exercises, etc.) | Flying Times Day | Night |
| 2/5/44 | 18.30 | J | F/o FORDE | ENGINEER | | CROSS COUNTRY & BOMBING. (FIRST ATTEMPT) | 2.20 | |
| 3/5/44 | 22.65 | E | " | " | | BOMBING — MONDIDIER (FRANCE) OP. NO. 8§ | | 4·00 |
| 5/5/44 | 16.25 | G | " | " | | LOCAL FLYING TURNED BACK BECAUSE OF ICING | ·40 | |
| 7/5/44 | 10.50 | F | " | " | | CROSS COUNTRY & BOMBING. | A/c u/s | |
| 9/5/44 | 00·55 | E | " | " | | BOMBING — MAINTES GASSICOURT (FRANCE) HIT BY FLAK. OP. NO. 91 | 2·00 | |
| 9/5/44 | 16·45 | F | " | " | | CROSS COUNTRY, BOMBING & AIR — SEA. FIRING. | 2.20 | |
| 9/5/44 | 0·203 | J | " | " | | BOMBING — HAINE (BELGIUM) SHOT UP BY FIGHTER (ME.110) BUT CLAIM A PROBABLE FOR REAR GUNNER D.F.M. FOR R/GUNNER OP. NO. 103 | | 3·00 |
| 10/5/44 | 10·50 | E | " | " | | CROSS COUNTRY & BOMBING | 1·40 | |
| 1/5/44 | 22·40 | O | " | " | | BOMBING — LOUVAIN (FRANCE) OP. NO. 113 | | 3·00 |
| 13/5/44 | 11·10 | 'H' | " | " | | CROSS COUNTRY. | 1·00· | |
| 14/5/44 | 11·85 | C | " | S | | BOMBING & AIR TO SEA FIRING | 2·00· | |
| | | | | | | Total Time | 96·40 | 77·05 |

28 Squadron records 35 Squadron... Victor's Pathfinder Lancaster posting, recording the downing of an enemy fighter (Bf110).

| Date | Aircraft Type & Number | Crew | Duty | Time Up | Time Down | Details of Sortie or Flight | References |
|---|---|---|---|---|---|---|---|
| | ME.333 (S). | F/L F.Watson. F/O K.S.Smith. F/O S.C.Scott. W/O Holland,L.G. F/O P.J.Pentelow. F/O Roe,V.A. F/S Cross,G. | Blind Marker | 17.28 | – | This aircraft is missing, nothing being heard from it after take off. | |
| | PB.676 (E). | F/L W.N.Cook. F/L A.B.Curtis. Sgt.Binns,G. F/E P.Coggan.(2nd A/B). F/O W.McDonald. P/O Garner,E. F/S Therault,D. Sgt.Varty,P. | Primary Visual Marker. | 17.28½ | 01.04 | 4x500 MC. 21.43½ hours. 13,000 feet. 155 T. 155 knots. 10/10ths strata cumulus. Identified by 4 clusters of R/G skymarkers. M/B heard very faintly ordering basement flight plan – later heard asking for skymarkers and instructing M/P to sky mark with overshoot. We descended to approximately 9,500 feet and cloud very thick. Bombed with 13 seconds overshoot on centre of skymarkers; these were disappearing into cloud and did not last long. Sky-marking was 3 clusters well concentrated and one under-shot to north. | |
| | PB.613 (P). | F/O E.Rigby. F/O C.J.A.Ramsey. F/O H.Breeze. F/O E.C.L.Cooths. Sgt.Cooper,R.F. P/O R.White. F/O D.J.Varney. | Blind Marker. | 17.30 | 01.16 | 1xCP.No.1 R/G. 2x250 TI.green. 2x350 TI.LB.green. 3xTP.No.5 4x1000 ANM.69. 1x500 MC. 21.43.48 hours. 17,000 feet. 170 T. 155 knots. 10/10ths strata cumulus, tops approximately 10/12000 feet. Identified and bombed on H2S. On run in, about six clusters of skymarkers green very well concentrated. M/D heard giving instructions but remained very poor but we heard him call for skymarkers and thought he said something else as well, so dropped everything to be on safe side. | |
| | PB.614 (G). | F/L H.Pettifer. F/O M.McMath. F/S Meredith,E.G. Flt./Off.S.Caddle. F/O K.Bullock. F/S Dent,E. F/S Judd,W.P. F/O T.Williamson. | Visual Centrer. | 17.33 | 01.30 | 21.52.30 hours. 16,000 feet. 163 T. 160 knots. 5x1000 ANM.65. 1x500 MC. 10/10ths stratus. Identified by red/green clusters, confirmed by H2S. On run up, saw about 4 markers/clusters of skymarkers in good concentration. These went down at 21.52 hours. They were not backed up very well. M/B's instructions heard to bomb centre of Wanganui flares with 12 seconds overshoot; later, there was only one odd flare left and then instructions received to bomb the glow. | |
| | ME.331 (F). | F/O W.G.Douglas. F/O A.Thompson. F/L W.M.Buck. F/O F.A.Stock.(2nd A/B). F/S Walters,M.L. F/S Marsh,G.L. F/S Andrew,S.J.H. F/O M.W.Hanham. | Visual Centrer. | 17.34 | 01.03 | 5x1000 ANM.65. 1x500 MC. 21.45 hours. 16,500 feet. 158 T. 155 knots. 10/10ths strata cumulus, tops 7-8000 feet. Identified by R/G flares checked by H2S. M/B was heard to ask for skymarking flares as we ran up and flares R/G fell about 21.42 hours. The first lot were backed up in good concentration and in good continuity, though about 21.45 there seemed a slight gap. There was no drift on the flares which merely ran downwind. | |

29 Squadron records 35 Squadron loss of Lancaster ME333 and the F. Watson crew on the Chemnitz raid. 'Failed to return' was a frequently used entry which hid all manner of outcomes. In this case it was the worst of all possibilities.

30 Runnymede paperwork for Victor's family.

ORDER OF CEREMONY
at the
UNVEILING OF THE

# RUNNYMEDE MEMORIAL

TO OFFICERS AND MEN OF THE

## AIR FORCES OF THE COMMONWEALTH

by

## HER MAJESTY THE QUEEN

Saturday, 17th October, 1953, at 2.30 p.m.

31 Runnymede paperwork for Victor's family.

---

Please bring this ticket with you.     8

MEDALS AND DECORATIONS may be worn with Civilian clothes.

REFRESHMENT facilities will be available adjacent to the Memorial.

LAYING OF WREATHS. Relatives are requested not to lay wreaths until the conclusion of the Ceremony.

PANEL

269

The number shown in the box above is that of the Panel within the Memorial on which may be found the name in which you are interested.

---

THE RUNNYMEDE MEMORIAL     N⁰ 4432

AIR FORCES OF THE COMMONWEALTH

*Admit Bearer to*

THE RELATIVES ENCLOSURE

*at the*

**CEREMONY OF UNVEILING**

*by*

HER MAJESTY THE QUEEN

*on Saturday, 17th October, 1953*

TICKET HOLDERS ARE REQUESTED TO BE IN THEIR PLACES BY TWO O'CLOCK
SEE OVER

32 Runnymede paperwork for Victor's family.

bring back and jettisoned the remainder in the designated spot in the North Sea on their way back. 635 Squadron who were sharing the raid with the Graveley contingent also had one returnee from this raid, the Westhorpe crew, who it was believed to have a similar engine problem.

## Ulm 17–18 December 1944

On the face of it, Ulm was a small city and not one that sprang to mind as a ready target. However it was home to several areas of great interest to the Allied high command. It housed a Magirus-Deutz vehicle assembly plant, a Kässbohrer vehicle plant as well as many other important factories on its industrial site producing a vast array of war materials. Nearby was a large barracks for the Wehrmacht, which included several hospitals where wounded soldiers were being restored to fighting fitness prior to being sent back to the front line. The town of Ulm itself housed many of the workers for the industrial sites in the area, and just to add to its interest as a target, it was home to one of the first Nazi concentration camps.

Situated between Stuttgart and Munich it was another long haul of nearly six and a half hours for the Watson crew and their fellow PFF Lancasters. All the 35 Squadron planes were airborne around 16.00, and homed in on the target area about 19.30. Victor's team did two runs over target, dropping their flares at 19.25 before going round again to drop their bombs just five minutes later.

There was a pretty comprehensive cloud cover, with a few gaps for a convenient glimpse of the target. Good concentration was reported for the TIs and fair for the bombing. Later reports showed reasonable damage to the vehicle plants, but a huge amount of destruction inflicted on the garrison and the virtual obliteration of the main town itself, rendering most of the twenty-five thousand workers homeless. There is no notification if any of the action was directed at the concentration camp, or its fences.

Two large explosions were seen in the area after the bombing and one report gave the sighting of the fires at the target site being visible at over one hundred and twenty miles away when the planes were on their homeward leg. 35 Squadron got all its crews home. Flak had been variable, fluctuating between very slight to heavy, but again there were no fighters to interfere with the operation and if there were any searchlights in the area they were certainly not being used.

## Koblenz 22–23 December 1944

It was obvious there would be no respite for anyone in the run up to the Christmas period. The Nazi regime was crumbling by the day and the Allied armies were closing in from every direction. Although this would be Victor's first visit to Koblenz, it was by no means the first time the PFF had paid a visit to the ancient city.

As a major transport crossing, situated at a point of multiple river crossings, railway marshalling yards and road junctions, it was a critical 'choke point' and as such received regular bombings and shellings and would continue to do so until it until it passed into Allied hands as the war came to a close.

For once the bomb load for ME335 was not recorded by the de-briefing officer, suffice to say it was more or less clear over target with just a little haze and it was identified both by H2S and visually by several of the attacking crews. A good bombing pattern was seen and the long haul home ended just after 21.45. All five planes on the raid from 35 Squadron returned intact.


## Nippes 24–25 December 1944

The marshalling yards at Nippes, or the Nippes district of Cologne, depending on which set of documents you read, was the next trip for Victor in ME335O-Oboe, but this time he had a different crew. For this trip he was teamed up with the Osmond crew and they set off as a PFF Supporter to mess up the Christmas of those needing the railway services that passed through the Nippes yards.

Sadly one of the Graveley planes, manned by the Kenyon crew barely made it into the air before it piled in and was a total loss. A second plane, the Roberts's crew lost one engine soon after take-off and needed to jettison part of the bomb load before it could continue with the raid. The Robert's plane then experienced some severe problems with its rudder system. The crew worked exceptionally hard that night to get their job done and get home.

But the raid was recorded as successful with explosions on the ground noted on a target that had been identified by DR, Gee and H2S by several different crews involved, even to the extent of the first snows of winter being noted by most of the crews when they were in the target area. All the PFF planes seemed to have a good bombing result. Dummy TIs and diversionary fires had been lit on the ground to try to confuse the inbound Lancasters, but it seems not to have worked at all on this occasion, and all the Graveley planes had a good result from their night's work.

For the first time in a long while all the returning Graveley Lancasters were diverted to alternative station for landing. 35 Squadron had an extra fifteen minutes flying time to RAF West Raynham in Norfolk on their return. The FIDO system at Graveley was not functioning as well as hoped on that occasion. As it was late on in the evening when they got to Raynham, Christmas morning would have to be delayed a few hours until they got back to Huntingdonshire.


## Gelsenkirchen 28–29 December

Gelsenkirchen had been visited by the Watson crew in ND916 just six weeks earlier, when the Nordstern synthetic oil plant had been attacked. This time further oil plant destruction was the aim, although the flattening of the town itself to deny housing for the workers of the Gelsenberg-Benzin AG was also part of the overall plan. There was a sub-camp of Buchenwald concentration camp in the area, supplying foreign slave labour to the fuel plants. This raid appeared to contribute to both the destruction of the plant and the denial of housing for the non-foreign section of the workforce.

The Watson crew took off from Graveley at a few minutes past four and arrived home a few minutes to nine. It was a long day for all the crews but not as long or as bad as some they had flown. The raid was reported by several crews as having scattered results as the full cloud undercast again meant bombing on H2S with no other references to help them with their accuracy. Nonetheless there were at least two very big explosions in the target area during the course of the attack, and the ensuing cloud column of dust and smoke from one of these explosions was observed by one of the departing crews when they were over one hundred miles distant from the site.

Later RAF reconnaissance photos were to show that at war's end over three quarters of the city of Gelsenkirchen had been completely flattened and rendered uninhabitable.

# 8

# Operations 1945

One mainstream school of thought echoing through the corridors of Whitehall in late 1944 had conjectured that the war in Europe could well be over before the New Year. Unfortunately its supporters had not taken into full account the depth of insanity that prevailed at the Berchtesgaden or in the Führer Bunker.

It was obvious to anyone with the smallest grip on reality that Nazi vengeance weapons or not, there was only going to be one conclusion to the conflict, it was merely a matter of how soon that could be achieved. Even so, instructions were issued to the German nation by Hitler to fight on. That said, it was then obviously still business as usual for Victor and the rest of the Pathfinder team at RAF Graveley, as it was for the whole of Bomber Command. But with the end in sight the whole Allied military machine would now push even harder than before, to bring the war to a timely conclusion.

## Ludwigshafen 2–3 January 1945

The first operation of the New Year for Victor was a return trip to Ludwigshafen, the scene of a PFF led raid just over two weeks earlier. They were allocated the job of Blind Secondary Marker in ME333 and were one of sixteen planes from 35 Squadron assembled for the raid.

Although designated a night raid, the PFF had reached the target area at 5.00 p.m. in good daylight by late afternoon, although of course it would take a while for the main bomber stream to do their bit, and it would be a night landing by the time they all got to return to their aerodromes. They all carried one 4,000-lb Minol bomb, plus others to make up the load, but the 4,000-lb Minol unit was the base ordnance of any load for 35 Squadron these days.

The weather was clear with some haze over target, so unsurprisingly it was reported as a good raid with several explosions noted and another set of fires started and left raging that Victor was again able to watch until they had flown a good eighty or ninety miles into their return leg home.

## Hanover 5–6 January 1945

Hanover City and its industrial area was deemed by their Lordships in Whitehall to be worthy of a visit by the boys of Bomber Command and their PFF vanguard. It was known to be well defended and not an easy target. True to expectation and briefing, heavy flak and a fighter presence was encountered on the raid and was particularly active in the target area. One crew in the raid reported in their post-raid interview that for the first time ever, their rear gunner had used up all his ammunition by the time he returned to base, he had been that busy defending their rear quarter from attacks.

Victor's crew were again allocated Blind Secondary Marker, a position they would now hold almost permanently. ME335O-Oboe was allocated to them for the night. Some 635 bombers were led on the raid by fourteen Oboe equipped LNSF Mosquitoes.

With almost a total cloud undercast in the target area at just 1,000 feet from the ground, the accuracy of the Mosquitoes and their sky markers would be essential for the success of this operation. However, the markers were not yet available when Victor and O-Oboe arrived and the Master Bomber requested they orbit for a few minutes until the TIs were in place. Later sections of the main bomber stream were redirected from using the Sky Markers to 'bomb on fire glow from target', so a reasonable measure of success must have been obvious to the Master Bomber from his position above the mayhem.

Several explosions were noted in and around the target during the course of the raid, further adding to the Master Bomber and the incoming crews' confidence. Unfortunately the persistent cloud cover prevented any real visual confirmation of this success.

Sadly the Potts crew in ME346 was listed as 'Failed to Return' in the final version of the 35 Squadron records.

## Hanau 6–7 January 1945

The major railway junction at Hanau was the next target for the Watson crew, although the tyre production and storage plant of W. C. Heraeus GmbH in the same town was a further tempting target that Bomber Command was somewhat keen to remove from the war effort. A third option on this sortie would be the industrial plants in the town that were working in precious metals and industrial diamonds. Hopefully the Watson crew having their only trip in ND676E-Easy would have some success; they could hardly miss getting one of the three in such a small area.

There were 482 bombers selected for the operation to Hanau. As usual they who would be led by two of the Mosquitos of the LNSF who were tasked to window ahead of the main bomber stream and drop the first of many bombs on the selected targets.

It was not quite all plain sailing for Victor's crew, as the brightness from the TIs dropped shortly before they arrived began flaring off the cloud formations over the target and made bomb aiming difficult and uncertain on their first run in to target. They had no option but to go round again to get it spot on. The heavy undercast prevented any realistic assessment of the raid at the time, though there was a general feeling from the returning crews was that it had been a pretty reasonable raid.

## Munich 7–8 January 1945

The city of Munich had many important industrial areas scattered in and around the municipal limits, particularly to the north and to the west. It was just too good a target opportunity the PFF to miss and for the Watson crew in ME335O-Oboe, it was the first real night raid for some time, with an estimated time over target of half past ten that evening. In actuality they were a mere two minutes adrift when they arrived.

Over the Sunday night of the seventh and into the early hours of the Monday 8 January the Watson crew were one part of several consecutive attacks which were launched on the city. The raging fires from the first bombing raid glowed through the dense cloud cover and served to act as in-built markers for those who followed behind. Victor's crew noted that the target was visible from sixty miles distant; such was the intensity and spread of the blaze.

Unsurprisingly the proliferation of Ack-Ack guns, searchlight batteries and night fighter squadrons located in the area surrounding the target were all understandably keen to get involved with the incoming British bombers. Fortunately luck was on the side of the Lancasters from 35 Squadron and all returned to Graveley safely just before dawn to a cold and frosty, winter's day.

The Watson crew were then rested for a few days after the Munich raid.

## Saarbrücken 13–14 January 1945

ME335 had been allocated to other crews during the Watson crew's time away from duty but fortunately it was still in one piece when they returned to Graveley and picking up where they left off, it was theirs for the night for the flight to Saarbrücken.

It was just one week on from their last operation and the weather situation had completely changed. The day that the railway marshalling yards were due to be attacked the winter weather had really kicked in and it was cold, clear and crisp. Accordingly from 18,000 feet the visibility was perfect, to such an extent that quite a few markers were brought back from the raid as 'un-used and un-needed'. The other very welcome change was the total lack of defences from either Ack-Ack guns, searchlights or fighters. It was a rather gentle return to work for Victor after a few days away from the war.

The marshalling yards in Saarbrücken were located in the north-west outskirts of the city and were large by any standards, being nearly a mile and a half long, running more or less north/south. 335's main load for this raid was five 2000-lb bombs.

It was a five-hour operation that ended at when they arrived home ... but not to Graveley on this occasion. At 20.40 that evening they landed at the fighter airfield at Tangmere in Sussex. Bad weather had made Graveley non-operational.

## Mersberg-Leuna 14–15 January 1945

Obviously the Leuna oil plant had been restored to some sort of working condition in the time that had passed since Victor's last visit; therefore a return trip to further disrupt the petrol production was called for. Bomber Command assembled 573 aircraft for the next raid on the plant which would start Saturday evening and be completed in the early hours of Sunday morning. It would be conducted in two separate waves. The Watson crew were allocated PB288U-Uncle and the role of Blind Marker in the second wave of the attack.

Unsurprisingly there was some flak over the target area as had been predicted at the briefing and just one lone fighter was seen. They had identified the target on the H2S, but elected to bomb on the fires from the first wave and achieved a good concentration.

None of the defences thrown at the incoming Lancasters seemed to greatly affect the standard of the PFF marking and bombing and the photo records showed that Bomber Command had achieved a remarkably successful raid. Several rather large explosions were noted at 23.58, 00.02, 00.03, and 00.05, and the tops of the visible cloud cover in the area changed from white to red as the raid progressed and the fires beneath took hold, huge columns of black smoke started to punch their way through the cloud tops into the clear upper skies. Clearly something of importance had been badly knocked about in the target zone, several thousand feet below the bomber stream.

Once again the Graveley contingent was forced to land away from home after the operation. This time the RAF Fighter Command station on the outskirts of Exeter in the far southwest was their host for the night.

## Zeitz 16–17 January 1945

Another manufacturing operation on the master list of synthetic oil plants that had attracted the attention of the strategists at Bomber Command was the Braunkohle-Benzin AG synthetic oil plant at Zeitz. With snow on the ground at Graveley and further snow showers forecast for most of the UK, there was always a question mark over this raid actually taking place.

In order to attempt to get the upper hand in the situation and stay operational, leave was cancelled as weather clearance crews were organised and put on standby to make sure only a really severe blizzard would close the Graveley runways. Fortuitously for the defenders that same winter weather in the target area had now produced a conveniently clear if slightly smoky visibility, making the work of the attacking bomber fleet that much easier.

The main bomber force seemed to nail the target pretty well and the Master Bomber was rewarded with a huge explosion just after quarter past ten. The smoke column from the burning plant was estimated to have risen some ten thousand feet into the winter sky.

On the return leg of the raid, the Watson crew noted that the fires from the Magdeburg raid, the second that night involving 35 Squadron, were visible from some 180 miles away. U-Uncle landed back at Graveley just after 01.30 on that Wednesday morning.

## Stuttgart 28–29 January 1945

If Zeitz had been a pretty successful and worthwhile operation, then Stuttgart raid a fortnight later was the complete opposite. 'A total waste of time and effort,' was one of the milder descriptions voiced by the returning crews. Other crew's versions employed a more basic tone of language.

Victor was back in the familiar turret of ME333S-Sugar for the operation to Stuttgart. However, 10/10 cloud cover, a malfunctioning H2S system and a bomb bay still packed full of ordnance when they returned to Graveley, probably sums up Victor's evening's work.

Most of the other planes on the raid also returned fully loaded and not surprisingly there were no substantial reports or raid results to talk about. Debriefing was incredibly quick and painless.

## Mainz 1–2 February 1945

PB305P-Peter was allocated to Victor and the Watson crew for their trip to Mainz that evening where more industrial areas were to receive the personal attentions of the Pathfinder Force and the wider Bomber Command. They were allocated the PFF Blind Secondary Marker position for this raid.

It was a somewhat smaller operation than those of recent days and saw 'just' 340 aircraft amassed for the attack. As was normal for these attacks, the whole bomber force bombed from around 18,000 feet. A full impenetrable undercast prevented any accurate de-brief, but most crews felt they had achieved a reasonable measure of success by using the H2S boxes confirmed by the subsequent glow from the target area. Several large explosions just after 19.30 would seem to have confirmed this further.

The Watson crew reported they delivered a good concentration of bombs, which seemed to tie in well with the results. It was another five and a half hour trip in total with P-Peter touching back down at RAF Graveley at a few minutes after 22.30.

The elation of a successful operation was enhanced when it was realised that all of the Lancasters of 35 Squadron had returned unscathed.

## Bonn 4–5 February 1945

Just a few days later it was Lancaster P-Peter that was again allocated to the Watson crew for another long haul trip, this time to Bonn. About half the 35 Squadron Lancasters were by now carrying a second Bomb Aimer, and although not specifically mentioned in the reports, it must be assumed that these Lancasters were now all H2S equipped, and their operators fully trained.

As the evening unfolded, it was shaping up to be a pretty 'interesting' sortie for several of the crews. The first crew to encounter difficulties was the D. J. Watson crew in PB257Y-Yoke who lost the starboard outer engine which started spitting sparks out of its exhaust as it ingested itself not long after gaining transit height. They had no option but to shut it down, feather the prop and drop out of the bomber stream. Standard procedure was then to head to the jettison area, unload anything live and limp back to Graveley on its three remaining engines. They arrived home a little before 21.00, just about the same moment that their colleagues were running in to target over Bonn.

About this same time, NG434T-Tommy managed to miss Bonn altogether and bombed Cologne by mistake. Then despite making the target overhead accurately and on time the Cook crew struggled to stay with a TI marker only to have it drop into the thick cloud layer and disappear from view before they could release their bombs. Several other crews reported the same difficulty, including Victor's. It was an exceedingly frustrating operation. Then to make matters worse, when they returned, it soon became obvious that the Johnson crew in 334 was missing.

Despite being unable to assess the final effects of the raid, the fact that this was another operation where the glow from the post-raid fires were visible for well over 100 miles, gave all the returning crews the hope that they had not totally wasted their evening's work.

## Goch 7–8 February 1945

Less than a mile and a half from the Dutch /German border just south of Nijmegen, Goch and its inhabitants would probably have taken the view that their community was far enough away from the main battle areas to avoid the attentions of RAF Bomber Command and the PFF. However on the night of Wednesday 7 February, there was a big surprise for them all and that all changed in a heartbeat.

What the good people of Goch and its near neighbour Kleve had not realised was that they were living in towns situated either side of a large impassable forested area that lay directly in the path of the advancing Allied armies and their push towards their immediate objective, the River Rhine. Putting things simply, both towns had to be pretty much flattened to prevent the German Army using them to hold up the planned advance.

Therefore the PFF were to lead twin raids on the unfortunate towns during the periods of darkness overnight on the 7 and 8 February to accomplish this. Sixteen planes would be required from 35 Squadron including the Watson crew in ME333 acting as Blind Illuminator again. Cloud cover that night varied from between 7/10 and 8/10 to almost total. Unsurprisingly the bombing was originally on the TIs for the first bombers to arrive, but later in the raid the Master Bomber changed the instruction again to one of aiming at the existing fires. This was undertaken until visibility over the target area was totally obliterated by smoke and dust and the Master Bomber decided he could do no more and aborted the rest of the raid.

So once again although the target or the remains of the target were not visible, there was reasonable ground for assuming the bombing had been successful. Operation times for 333 were:

Take-off: 19.43.
Time over target: 22.24.
Landing: 00.28½.

By now the practice of timing landings and take-offs to ¼ minutes seemed to have fortunately been forgotten at 35 Squadron, and records showed all were recorded to within the minute, and that only Victor's plane that night was one that somehow attracted the odd half-minute notation against their entry.


## Politz 8–9 February 1945

Two more synthetic oil plants were the targets for the raids on the night of 8 February. 35 Squadron including Victor's crew were allocated places on the raid on Politz, but not on the other that was planned to attack the plant at Wanne-Eickel which would be handled by other PFF squadrons. This was one of several such attacks on that plant in just a few weeks.

Some 475 bombers formed the main bomber stream which made the long trip to Politz. With clear winter skies helping considerably with their efforts they bombed the oil plant in two distinct waves.

The Hydrierwerke Politz AG plant at Politz was the biggest of the German synthetic oil plants and was responsible for producing something like 700,000 metric tons of petrol a year. It was simply un-acceptable for the Allies to leave it standing and able to operate.

ME333 with Victor and the Watson Crew aboard were again allocated the Blind Secondary Marker role for this trip. It was to be one of the longer operations on Bomber Command's immediate agenda and would have the crews airborne for just over eight hours.

They bombed from 15,000 feet and paraphrasing one of the reports ... 'Good marking, Good bombing, Good results'. During the raid there were a number of reports of several TIs being seen a number of miles to the south and east. They were all believed to be dummy markers placed deliberately by the defenders to create confusion in the minds of the attacking bombers. On this occasion at least, it did not work. It had been a long, long day for everyone.

## Operation Thunderclap

*Operation Thunderclap* was devised by the Air Ministry to put further pressure on the Nazi leadership to bring the war to a halt. At the request of the Russian leadership, the Air Ministry would instruct Bomber Command to commence an intense and sustained bombing campaign against major German cities once the Red Army crossed the borders into German territory. It was planned from the very top with Winston Churchill himself having an active hand in its planning, as it was considered that important.

The campaign was devised so that a 'Second Internal Front' would come into play once the Red Army reached a predetermined point of its attack on Berlin. Thus *Operation Thunderclap* was planned to commence on 13 February with a daylight raid on Dresden to be undertaken by the USAAF. However, bad weather prevented this from taking place, so as it turned out, the night raid by RAF that same evening was the first to lead into that city.

The USAAF then followed up with three more raids including a separate attack on the rail system including the marshalling yards. This was designed to hamper escape out of the city and to slow down relief services entering the zone of destruction. Further the USAAF tasked the bombers' Mustang fighter escorts to drop out of high level formation and carry out strafing runs on the streets of Dresden to maximise the confusion that the raid had been planned to create. If successful this was to be the prototype for a whole host of *Operation Thunderclap* raids that would also target Chemnitz and Berlin. That was of course until the proximity of the Russian ground troops made it impractical to continue.

After the tactical success of the Dresden raid Churchill was extremely delighted and personally encouraged Bomber Command's C-in-C, Sir Arthur Harris to rethink the RAF bombing strategy and instructed them to include Leipzig on the list of the main cities to be targeted by the operation. Smaller targets were to be added to *Operation Thunderclap*, as and when the opportunity arose.

It was during this short break for the Watson crew that Flying Officer Pentelow joined them and became a permanent member.

## Dresden 13–14 February 1945

35 Squadron had two attacks to help lead that night, one to Bohlen and one to Dresden. Dresden city itself was the target of the attack that Victor and 333 were scheduled to attend. It was the site of the much-discussed firestorm that developed in the wake of the attack.

HE Bombs and Incendiary Bombs were dropped on a ratio of approximately two to one and were the lethal cocktail that started the fires. This mixture of explosives and incendiary devices reacted with the highly combustible wooden buildings in the city centre. Then the local wind characteristics conspired in creating the fire vortex that produced all the carnage to the city population.

It is also understood that the authorities had provided woefully insufficient air-raid shelters for the city population and it was therefore inevitable that many domestic basements and cellars had been pressed into use during the raid. The greater majority of these cellars were housed under the wooden buildings themselves, and as such were of course entirely inadequate, in most cases doing more harm than good.

Codenamed *Operation Thunderclap* to emphasise its importance, this was the initial raid of a series of attacks under the same name aimed specifically at large conurbations of German factory workers. The Allied High Command had hoped the wholesale destruction of the housing and the displacement of the civilian work force would bring the Nazi leadership to its senses and convince them it was time to lay down their arms.

Sadly it was not yet to be. In fact this raid was used, with some considerable degree of success, by Josef Goebbels the Nazi propaganda minister, to plant doubt in the minds of the Allies as to the justness of their own cause. Massively exaggerated claims of death and destruction were publicised. The number of casualties reported to Goebbels' Propaganda Ministry appeared to be the local, official figures, simply multiplied by ten.

With their participation in this raid, the crew of ME333S-Sugar was embarking on what was almost certainly the longest operation of their Pathfinder Force career. When their Lancaster lifted off at 22.02 on that Tuesday evening, their landing at Graveley was still a whisker over eight and a half hours away, well into the daylight of the following morning.

Victor and his fellow RAF crews would drop some 2,600 tons of ordnance in two waves during that one raid alone. The B17s and B24s of the USAAF then followed up the next day with a further mission that added 771 tons of explosives being targeted into an already devastated city. Incredibly, even after this overwhelming show of force, the German leadership still somehow failed to grasp the reality of the situation.

In all senses of the word, for the Pathfinder Force, Bomber Command and the wider objectives of the Allies' war efforts, it was an extremely successful operation.

## Chemnitz 14–15 February 1945

One attack, but in two parts were planned for the city of Chemnitz that evening also under the banner of *Operation Thunderclap*. It was planned in two waves approximately three hours apart. The first wave had just over 600 aircraft in it and the second wave a lot smaller with 'just' 250.

The Watson crew were scheduled as part of the second attack. Unfortunately a complete cloud undercast made the bombing fairly scattered, on both attacks. Interestingly the first wave experienced no flak but several sustained fighter attacks, yet the second wave saw no fighters but experienced some reasonably heavy flak.

The load for 333 that night was purely TIs and Markers, thus when the Master Bomber decided to use sky markers because of the prevailing weather conditions, the Watson crew had a bomb bay full of un-required markers so they had no option but to bring them back to Graveley for use another day.

One PFF plane from 635 Squadron in the first wave of the attack was the reported victim to one of the new German jet fighters, the Messerschmitt Me262.

## Dortmund 20–21 February 1945

This was again an attack in the city itself and the factories in its industrial areas supporting the Nazi war effort. The 35 Squadron briefing warned of heavy flak and very active fighter activity in the area. As it turned out, this was a 100 per cent accurate prediction and the German defences were as lively as predicted.

The weather was not the best for the PFF force or the main bomber stream that had just over 500 aircraft at its disposal for this operation. Fourteen LNSF Oboe Mosquitos windowed ahead of the Lancasters and as usual did the initial target marking. The Watson crew had ME333S-Sugar again and were designated Blind Secondary Marker. They were loaded with the usual 4,000-lb bomb and five 1,000-lb bombs, plus markers, for the five and a half hour operation. The crews of 35 Squadron could almost be forgiven for thinking that the war was becoming a bit routine.

Despite a somewhat shaky start to the bombing runs, TI and bombing concentration was seen to tighten up during the course of the attack, and the post-raid photographic reconnaissance showed good results with some areas of the city totally obliterated. Many of the rear gunners on the raid again noted as they flew away that the glow from the fires was visible from almost 100 miles. That said, it was not all a one-way street on this occasion and although 35 Squadron got all its crews back, five bombers from the main bomber force fell victims to the very active and experienced night fighters operating in the area.

## Duisburg 21–22 February 1945

Duisburg was another afternoon raid for Victor, S-Sugar and the usual team. As with the previous operation it was almost becoming predictable. Thin cloud meant the target was sometimes visible to the Watson crew and certainly some estimate of the raids effectiveness was possible before the last plane left for home. The crew in S-Sugar had bombed on H2S due to the sporadic cloud undercast occasionally blocking the view. It seemed to work well enough for them.

Their operational times read:

Take off 22.19.
Over Target 01.02.
Landed 03.23.

Fortunately for them all, a somewhat shorter raid than many of the others they had flown in the last few days. Sadly they lost two planes on this one raid. The Tropman crew in ME367 and their old friend ME335 with the J. J. Osmond crew aboard were both listed as failed to return. Victor had flown with the Osmond crew as a volunteer just two months earlier on Christmas Eve. They had not lost two crews on one raid for quite a long while and it was a nasty wake-up call.

## Essen 23 February 1945

Essen was another afternoon raid for the contingent from 35 Squadron, and quite a trouble free one at that. As they ran in towards Essen at 18,000 feet, the cloud over the target area was in a non-co-operative mood again and so the Gee and H2S systems were put to good use to deliver their bomb loads. Victor noticed that the crews of a group of Halifaxes behind them homed in on their run and used 333's release position to drop their own ordnance on the target. Cheeky but effective.

As before with these afternoon operations, Victor and the crew were back at Graveley in time for a swift half before dinner.

## Mainz 27 February 1945

Despite the fact that the war was rapidly drawing to a close, there was no let-up in the internal pressure on all areas of German industry to produce war materials. The industrial plants in and around the city of Mainz, just to the west of Frankfurt, were no exception. Soldiers and tanks may well have been pouring back to the German borders from both the Eastern Front and from the Allied onslaught in the west, but the weird Nazi logic was to keep producing guns and bullets. This, despite the fact that there was no one to use them locally, and not enough fuel to get them to the soldiers further away, who actually needed them.

The LNSF provided sixteen Mosquitos to lead a formation of a further 400 or more heavy bombers. The clear skies were useful to the attacking formation, but with the lower temperatures encountered, several of the Lancasters reported that they had experienced icing problems and were forced to fully utilise the planes' on board de-icing systems to keep going. The strong winds which added to the wind chill factor on the ground also gave navigators and pilots a good work out keeping the fleet on track and on time. At the briefing earlier, no one had said it was going to be an easy raid.

The flak over target was heavy, but it looked as if the previous attacks on the synthetic oil plants were having their effect and there were no fighters to worry Victor or his opposite number in the Lancaster's mid upper turret. They had to assume there was not enough petrol available to the Luftwaffe to mount any sort of defence. Obviously the strategy of hitting the synthetic oil plants hard was starting to hit home.

## Mannheim 1 March 1945

The Watson crew were in ME333 for the eleventh time for the raid on Mannheim. More industrial manufacturing plants were targeted for their visit on 1 March. Led by sixteen LNSF Mosquitos, who as normal Windowed ahead of the main bomber stream, some 478 planes from Bomber Command were tasked with the job of flattening as much of the target area as possible. There was a complete cloud undercast when the Mosquitoes got there, and the situation was not to change for the duration of the raid. The operation was once again planned by Pathfinder Headquarters to operate from 18,000 feet. The cloud in the area rose to 12,000 feet so marking for the main force was done by Sky Markers. When Victor's plane arrived, the scene was not quite set, so the Master Bomber ordered them to orbit for a couple of minutes and then come in to make their attack.

The first attack wave was only fair in its accuracy and concentration, but the second wave appeared to have nailed the target exactly and achieved some really excellent results. However, with a reasonably broad target area to go at, even the 'fair' results claimed for the raid as a whole were certainly blowing up something of use and no doubt contributing to the overall success of the day.

ME333 had been loaded with ten 1,000-lb HE bombs and markers for the run to Mannheim that afternoon. ME333 had recorded operational times as follows.

Take off: 12.28½.
Time over target: 15.08½.
Landing: 17.57.

## Chemnitz 5–6 March 1945

On 5 March, just three weeks after notification of his last promotion, their Navigator Ken Smith received his second promotion. He was now Flight Lieutenant Smith. Just four days later on the came the news that Pilot, Flight Lieutenant Watson was now Squadron Leader Watson and that Flying Officer Scott had been also been promoted and was now Flight Lieutenant Scott. Not surprisingly they were a bit busy with the war so the traditional celebrations for such occasions in the mess and local pubs would have to wait.

A return trip to Chemnitz was planned for Monday 5 March. Some 760 planes were allotted to take part in the raid against the Chemnitz railway marshalling yards. The yards took on extra importance this time as the Germans were known to be planning a large reinforcing operation to rush more men to the eastern front. With the front now ever closer to Berlin it was even more important to try to ease the load on the Red Army by cutting off the ability for the Wehrmacht to bring forward troop reserves.

With Chemnitz located rather close to the Swiss-German border this was to be a very long raid of some eight and a half hours from chock-to-chock. To make it harder, intelligence indicated a particularly heavy flak concentration in the area. The Met Flight boys had forecast a total cloud cover with layers of wispy cloud likely even above the bombers operational height of 18,000 feet. Neither the weather or defensive forecasts were wrong, but the major surprise of the operation was that thirty or more RAF bombers were to be lost on this one raid. When advised of this unexpectedly high figure, C-in-C of Bomber Command, Sir Arthur Harris was reported to be both upset and extremely displeased.

The Watson crew again aboard their regular Lancaster E333S-Sugar, was amongst those who did not make it back to base. It was believed their plane was hit by flak in the target area and plummeted to earth in what is now an allotment area, just off Fredrick Engles Strasse in Chemnitz. It would appear that Navigator Ken Smith had managed to escape the doomed plane but at too low an altitude, or that he had been thrown clear on impact. Sadly he had not survived either. All the members of the seven-man crew were buried in a collective grave in Chemnitz. Victor had flown his last sortie. Had it been completed it would have been his ninety-eighth combat operation.

Needless to say the operation had started off as all the others before it. The Watson crew were no doubt looking forward to celebrating the various recent crew promotions and of course the next major crew achievement, that of Victor's one hundredth raid, in a couple of days' time. Unusually there was nothing recorded in the squadron logs regarding their bomb load that night. They took off on schedule just before 17.30 that evening and were literally never seen again.

Victor's CGM (Conspicuous Gallantry Medal) was announced in the *London Gazette* just a few weeks later on 13 April 1945.

# 9

# *Mission Accomplished*

Historians the world over have always held a variety of conflicting opinions on the moment in time when the Nazi Regime actually 'lost' the war. For some it had to be Stalingrad, some the Battle of Britain and for others either D-Day or perhaps even the loss of Italy to the Allied powers. Regardless of what pundits may discuss now, back in mid-1944, there was a general feeling in Allied High Command that the Allied war machine really had the enemy on the run and that they were now *en route* to victory. This feeling permeated down throughout the command chain, even if the exact date of the war's end could not yet be foretold by anyone. In many ways it was down to how quickly the Russian troops on the ground could smash their way into Berlin and reach the Chancellery and/or the Führer Bunker.

D-Day had long since come and gone, and the push inland from the invasion beaches of France was solidly under way. The huge Russian army was making great strides all along the Eastern Front, and despite the terrible cost in men and machinery was relentlessly pushing the battered and exhausted Wehrmacht back towards the German borders. The Allies' drive up through Italy and from the south of France was also well under way, and the occasional thought that it perhaps could all be finished in 1944 had crossed the minds of some of the more optimistic leaders along the corridors of power.

However, it was not to be and again the harsh winter months in central Europe intervened to help prolong the ultimate collapse of Hitler's perverted dream of world domination. This in itself presented no change of plan whatsoever for Victor, or any of the aircrew in any of the Pathfinder Force. Every sortie over enemy territory for the PFF was very much 'business as usual'. The strategic bombing of the crumbling German industrial base was all aimed at bringing the conflict swiftly to an end and saving as many lives from being wasted as it possibly could.

The flying duties for all Bomber Command crews continued unabated day after day and week after week. Their brief always remained the same, to keep smashing at the German infrastructure until the Nazi leadership realised that there was no way back and cried 'enough'. Sadly with a seriously unhinged leader who was living in a drug-induced world of total denial and who had surrounded himself with a sycophantic inner circle of advisors, that situation would take until the late spring of 1945, to arrive. It was only in fact a few days after Hitler had committed suicide, that the proverbial penny finally dropped, and some small semblance of sanity overtook the remains of the ruling Nazi hierarchy. This fortunately enabled the surrender documents to be signed, and the guns fall silent; only then could Europe wearily collapse into a welcome and long awaited peace.

Victor and his PFF colleagues had led the way for Bomber Command to systematically destroy the vast German industrial machine, as well as take the occasional swipe at the Nazi military along the way. Aided by the USAAF's daylight raids, they doggedly kept attacking and flattening the industry and infrastructure that had fed the Nazi dictatorship with the weapons and machinery that were essential for it to pursue its World War. This in turn, with the increasing dominance of RAF Fighter Command in the air, had allowed the Allied ground troops to move forward on all fronts to free the occupied territories and push into Germany to destroy the powerbase of the Nazi Party. This had always been their unflinching aim and it never changed; so that is precisely what the Pathfinders did, day after day and step after step. Sadly for Victor and many of his colleagues in the PFF and the wider Bomber Command, the final push would come too late and they would not be around to see it and enjoy that euphoric day.

Looking back, the accomplishments of the whole of Bomber Command and the PFF in particular had been amazing, not only in their own right as a strategic bomber force but also as a flexible tactical support to the Allied troops on the ground. It is particularly outstanding when the results are evaluated in conjunction with the level of equipment that was supplied to the crews to carry out the job.

Although one could claim that many facets of the PFF equipment were truly 'state of the art' for their time, it was not until the latter stages of the war that some of the equipment started to become equal to the task the Pathfinders were being asked to perform. What they had previously lacked in technical wizardry, they generally made up for with training, their own skill, bravery and sheer bloody determination.

The PFF daily raid reports are littered with references to equipment failures ranging from the tiresomely tedious to the real heavyweight show-stopping disasters. Not many squadrons' reports got completed without reporting the fact that one or two aircraft returned to base with fewer engines running than the designers deemed preferable, or with bits missing from the plane that the crew would have preferred to have remained attached. It is also worth noting here that on many occasions a seriously disgruntled enemy often had a thing or two to say about what the RAF was getting up to.

Many years on from those dark days of war, it is hard to imagine what Victor would have done with the remainder his life had he just made it through those last few weeks. Most certainly he could have opted to stay in the RAF, although 'tail gunner aircrew' was definitely not a long-term peacetime career, but then re-training to another trade was always an option, either as aircrew or ground crew. The idea of going back to farming, on the face of it, looks an incredibly dull option for someone with Victor's nature and a recent history of dangerous and rather lively wartime experiences. Then there was of course always the classic option of doing 'something completely different'.

A return to his home city of Norwich has to be considered a very distinct possibility if the civilian route was to have been his peacetime choice. The fact that he returned to Norfolk several times on leave and obviously liked to spend time with his brothers and sisters, also tends to back that as a rather strong option. It is not known if any of the other parts of the country where he was posted when he was in the RAF ever struck a chord with Victor. If it did, there appears to be no mention of it in any of his private paperwork. Needless to say we will never know, as sadly that option was denied him, as it was to the many millions of victims of Hitler's insanity.

He would never have known the gratitude of his fellow countrymen and the world as a whole, for his part in ridding the world of the Nazis, nor felt the satisfaction of finally seeing the end of such a heinous regime. He obviously loved his job, and he was known to do it exceptionally well. Once Christmas 1944 had passed he must have known full well from the way his part of the war was playing out, that the Allies were now totally dominant and would fairly soon crush the German military machine and win the war. Perhaps to Victor that would have been reward enough.

Victor's name and those of his colleagues in the Watson crew are remembered on Panel 285 of the Runnymede Memorial.

# 10

# The Paperwork for a Hero

During the course of the Second World War, tens of thousands of RAF aircrew from all over Britain, the Commonwealth and wider world gave their lives fighting for their country, for a cause that they believed to be right or to free their country from Nazi tyranny. In each and every case, the UK Government through the Casualty Branch of the Air Ministry were responsible for advising the next of kin specified on the airman's records of that sad event.

The standard procedure was to advise the next of kin when the plane was overdue, first by telegram then by a follow up confirmation letter, usually by the squadron adjutant. It was then, after it was obvious that the plane had not landed away from its base or been found in UK territory but not where it should be, that the next phase of the process kicked in and the 'missing in action' letters started. Notification of POW status or a successful 'escape and evade' scenario frequently took months to confirm, so usually at about that stage it was the practice for the squadron or station CO to write personally to the immediate next of kin. This was the job, which was thought by the greater majority of serving officers to be the worst of all duties they were asked to do in the RAF. It was made much harder if it was almost certain from other aircraft reports there was no hope at all for the crew.

After all notifications had occurred and due time had elapsed, there then followed the well-practiced procedure for the return of that airman's personal belongings and the recovery of outstanding RAF property, including the settling of any 'official' debts. The return of the airman's belongings, regardless of the how, when and why of his death, happened via the RAF Central Depository at Colnbrook. Finally the repatriation of the body (if possible) and everything else that was needed to 'tidy-up' that airman's affairs. If the body was available in the UK, then it was standard procedure for a contingent of his squadron to be sent to represent the RAF, at the funeral. These procedures happened hundreds of times every week for the Air Force alone. Needless to say the Army and the Navy both had need of similar operations of their own.

It was a thankless and relentless routine procedure handled by clerks who had to process the information in that totally impersonal, 'tick in the box' way or they would never have been able to do their job at all. The most difficult letters to write were the ones that came from the COs and colleagues of the airman concerned. They were the ones who had to start by saying, 'Dear Mrs XXXXX, I'm sorry to have to tell you ...' In Lancaster squadrons because of the crew numbers, these letters were inevitably written in batches of seven or eight.

It is hard for us, many decades on in a more peaceful world, to imagine the situation in which the relatives of downed aircrew found themselves. Initially it was a 'failed to return' telegram, then a 'missing presumed dead' notification, then the final 'officially dead' letter. It was also a sequence that can also be easily seen on the internal RAF documentation, including the very authoritarian, 'do not talk to the press' leaflet. Each official notification was bound to send further shockwaves and hurt through the immediate family, who were always hoping against hope that there would be some vestige of good news and their loved one was in hospital, recovering, returning from Europe, or even a POW in Germany. All outcomes distinctly better than the life changing, 'We regret to inform you', letter that so many families received.

In Victor's case we actually have a German housewife, a Frau Sayfert who lived in Chemnitz, to thank for finally putting the last pieces of Victor's story together for us. When some years after the war had ended, the RAF's Missing Research and Enquiry Service were allowed into the Russian sector of Germany to start the official post-war investigations and repatriation of identified bodies. At this point, she came forward with the final part of the story and the proof, in the form of Ken Smith's Identity Card, that the crew of S-Sugar were indeed interred in a communal grave in the city cemetery in Chemnitz. Some exhumation was allowed by the Russian authorities which confirmed that the communal grave also contained the body of an airman from another Lancaster also lost on the same raid.

Unsurprisingly this gave rise to one school of speculation that the two planes may have touched while over target and this subsequently brought them both down so close together. It was certainly not an unknown situation in the heat of battle. It did also confirm that Victor's crew in S-Sugar had indeed completed their bombing raid, as the wreckage was reported by Frau Seyfert to have fallen in the allotments on Fredrik Engle Strasse in the western suburbs of Chemnitz, on a route that matched their course to return home. The fact that there was no subsequent explosion was now proof enough that the bomb load had not been on board when the plane crashed and must therefore have already been dropped.

It is pretty certain that the relatives of all aircrew members knew only too well that their menfolk had willingly volunteered to train for, and undertake a very dangerous task and that it was one that they all understood that they may never return from. Unfortunately it was true to say that at that time almost everyone's lives were in one way or another more at risk than before the start of the war. It is really impossible looking back to gauge how much any of this helped when that fateful day and the official buff telegram actually arrived; probably very little, if at all.

For most people today the official Second World War procedure of notification of MIA through to KIA and its immediate aftermath is something they probably only get to read about in a piecemeal fashion in books like this, or view in public libraries or museums across the country. Over half a century on from the conflict, it is somewhat rare for a complete set of these documents to remain together.

Fortunately, despite Victor's fractured family situation as a youngster, both the official paperwork relating to his death in service (included here in its entirety) and a good selection of the private letters from that time, have been carefully kept and preserved by the family he was just starting to rediscover. Other material located after the war has been methodically added to the file as it came to light. Thus we have the original documents as both an integral part of Victor's life story and as a collection of wartime military documents available for its wider historical interest that will hopefully be a useful source of information and study for historians and students of that era.

It is how Victor's family wanted it to be.

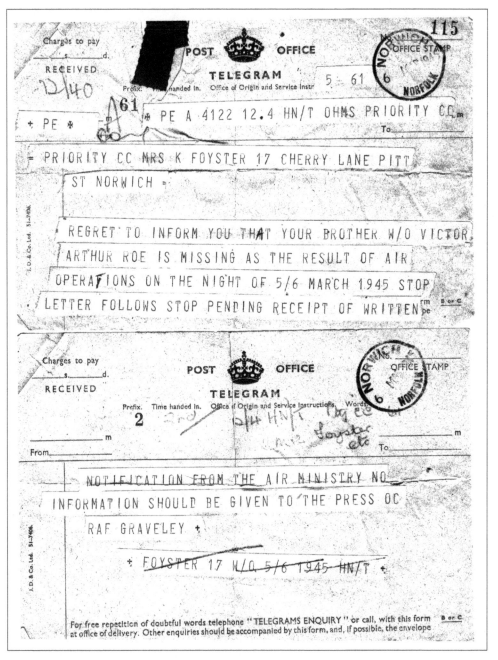

POST OFFICE

TELEGRAM      5 - 61      115

Prefix. Time handed in. Office of Origin and Service Instr

61      PE A 4122 12.4 HN/T OHMS PRIORITY CC

+ PE *                                          To

= PRIORITY CC MRS K FOYSTER 17 CHERRY LANE PITT
ST NORWICH =

REGRET TO INFORM YOU THAT YOUR BROTHER W/O VICTOR
ARTHUR ROE IS MISSING AS THE RESULT OF AIR
OPERATIONS ON THE NIGHT OF 5/6 MARCH 1945 STOP
LETTER FOLLOWS STOP PENDING RECEIPT OF WRITTEN

POST OFFICE

TELEGRAM

Prefix. Time handed in. Office of Origin and Service Instructions. Words
2

From                                          To

NOTIFICATION FROM THE AIR MINISTRY NO
INFORMATION SHOULD BE GIVEN TO THE PRESS OC
RAF GRAVELEY +

+ FOYSTER 17 W/O 5/6 1945 HN/T +

1 The telegram. The first official notification that all is not well and all your worst fears are about to come true. For most, even worse news would soon follow.

Royal Air Force,
Graveley,
Hunts.

Ref: 35S/C.68/175/P.1.          6th March, 1945.

Dear Mrs. Foyster,

        It is with profound regret that I find
it my unhappy task to confirm the telegram you will have
received informing you that your Brother is missing as
the result of air operations.

        As Tail Gunner of his aircraft, he and
his crew took off at twenty eight minutes past five on the
evening of 5th March, 1945 to attack Chemnitz, and nothing
further was heard from them, so it is impossible for me
to give the reason for their failure to return, but I do
assure you that any information received will be passed to
you immediately. The usual source of news is the International Red Cross Committee who advise Air Ministry, they
in turn sending you a telegram. In other cases, where the
aircrew concerned is a prisoner of war in enemy hands,
frequently a letter is received direct by the Next-of-Kin
prior to this telegram.

        Having completed an exceptionally large
number of sorties, your Brother had obtained for himself
an excellent operational record and had repeatedly proved
himself to be absolutely fearless. His determination and
keenness to fly against the enemy on all possible occasions
was outstanding and it will not be easy to replace him.

        There are, however, always a proportion
of missing crews who escape by parachute or make a forced
landing and I, the Squadron as a whole and your Brother's

                                  P.T.O.

2 The letter of confirmation. Very rarely it would confirm a landing away from base, a parachute escape or even a POW status. Most however were like this.

brother aircrew share your impatience for the good news
that he is safe though a prisoner of war. Meanwhile, we
wish you to know that you have our deepest sympathy in
this period of anxiety.

        Attached to this letter is a list of the
Next-of-Kin of the members of the crew. Should you wish
to write to any of them, please send your letters to me
addressed, stamped and sealed and I will arrange for them
to be forwarded.

        Your Brother's kit and private property is
now being attended to by the Effects Officer. It is the
regulation that this is forwarded to a Standing Committee
of Adjustment, R.A.F. Central Depository, Colnbrook,
Buckinghamshire, who will communicate with you in due course
submitting the inventories of personal property.

        Please do not hesitate to ask my assistance on
any points not covered in this letter.

                Yours sincerely,

                (J.J.F. LeGood).
                Wing Commander,
                Squadron Commander.

Mrs. K. Foyster,
17, Cherry Lane,
Pitt Street, Norwich.

**BUCKINGHAM PALACE**

The Queen and I offer you
our heartfelt sympathy in your
great sorrow.

We pray that your country's
gratitude for a life so nobly
given in its service may bring
you some measure of consolation.

*George R.I*

Mrs. K. Foyster.

3 The condolence letter from
The Palace.

---

**The Royal Air Force Benevolent Fund.**

PATRON : H.M. THE KING.
PRESIDENT : H.R.H. THE DUCHESS OF KENT.
CHAIRMAN : THE RT. HON. LORD RIVERDALE, G.B.E.

Telephone No.: HOVE 3392.
All Communications to be addressed to the Secretary.

| Our Reference | MJ/AMS 275. |
| Your Reference | |

EATON HOUSE,
14, EATON ROAD,
HOVE, SUSSEX.

12th March, 1945.

Mrs. K. Foyster,
17 Cherry Lane,,
Pitt Street,
Norwich.

Dear Madam,

The Council of the Royal Air Force Benevolent Fund have
learnt with much regret that your brother is reported missing,
and I am asked to convey to you their very sincere sympathy.

My Council, in their desire to assist dependants in every
possible way, have decided that however unlikely the need of
assistance from this Fund may appear to be, we should at least
write and get into touch with dependants or next-of-kin to see
whether anything can be done financially or otherwise.

If there is anything I can do to help please let me know,
and if this savours of intrusion, I hope you will forgive in
the light of the above explanation.

Yours truly,

Squadron Leader,
Secretary.

4 The 'system' swings into
action for the Watson crew. Back
at Graveley a new crew would
already be fitting in to squadron
life.

# ADVICE TO THE RELATIVE
# OF A MAN WHO IS MISSING

In view of the official notification that your relative is missing, you will naturally wish to hear what is being done to trace him.

The Service Departments make every endeavour to discover the fate of missing men, and draw upon all likely sources of information about them.

A man who is missing after an engagement may possibly be a prisoner of war. Continuous efforts are made to speed up the machinery whereby the names and camp addresses of prisoners of war can reach this country. The official means is by lists of names prepared by the enemy Government. These lists take some time to compile, especially if there is a long journey from the place of capture to a prisoners of war camp. Consequently " capture cards " filled in by the prisoners themselves soon after capture and sent home to their relatives are often the first news received in this country that a man is a prisoner of war. That is why you are asked in the accompanying letter to forward at once any card or letter you may receive, if it is the first news you have had.

Even if no news is received that a missing man is a prisoner of war, endeavours to trace him do not cease. Enquiries are pursued not only among those who were serving with him, but also through diplomatic channels and the International Red Cross Committee at Geneva.

The moment reliable news is obtained from any of these sources it is sent to the Service Department concerned. They will pass the news on to you at once, if they are satisfied that it is reliable. It would be cruel to raise false hopes, such as may well be raised if you listen to one other possible channel of news, namely, the enemy's broadcasts. These are listened to by official listeners, working continuously night and day. The few names of prisoners given by enemy announcers are carefully checked. They are often misleading, and this is not surprising, for the object of the inclusion of prisoners' names in these broadcasts is not to help the relatives of prisoners, but to induce British listeners to hear some tale which otherwise they could not be made to hear. The only advantage of listening to these broadcasts is an advantage to the enemy.

The official listeners can never miss any name included in an enemy broadcast. They pass every name on to the Service Department concerned. There every name is checked, and in every case where a name can be verified, the news is sent direct to the relatives.

There is, therefore, a complete official service designed to secure for you and to tell you all discoverable news about your relative. This official service is also a very human service, which well understands the anxiety of relatives and will spare no effort to relieve it.

21527    37345 Q 2916  5,000  11/44   K.H.K.   **Gp. 8/8**

5 The primary Government advice note.

Ref:
CY/CA/202/213/P.3.

R.A.F. Station,
Graveley,
Hunts.

11th March, 1945.

Dear Mrs. Foyster,

As the Officer supervising the disposal of your
brother's effects, may I be permitted to offer you my very sincere
sympathy.

In accordance with Air Ministry instructions the
effects duly assembled will shortly be forwarded to the Standing
Committee of Adjustment, Central Depository, R.A.F. Colnbrook, Slough,
Bucks., who will communicate with you as soon as the official checking
formalities have been completed by them.

A Post Office Savings Bank Book CURTISDEN GN No.689
was found amongst the effects, and will be forwarded to Air Ministry,
Department Accounts 13, Worcester, for their attention.

Yours sincerely,

*[signature]* F/Lt.
For Group Captain, Commanding,
R.A.F. Station, Graveley.

Mrs. K. Foyster,
17, Cherry Lane,
Pitt Street,
Norwich.

6  The 'system' is in full swing and takes over.

Telephone No.: GERRARD 9234

Trunk Calls and }
Telegraphic Address : } "AIR MINISTRY," LONDON

P. 430140/5/P.4.A.2.

AIR MINISTRY,

(Casualty Branch),

73-77 OXFORD STREET,
LONDON, W.1.

19 March, 1945.

Madam,

      I am commanded by the Air Council to express to you their great regret on learning that your brother, Warrant Officer Victor Arthur Roe, D.F.M., Royal Air Force, is missing as the result of air operations on the night of 5th/6th March, 1945, when a Lancaster aircraft in which he was flying as rear gunner set out to bomb Chemnitz and was not heard from again.

      This does not necessarily mean that he is killed or wounded, and if he is a prisoner of war he should be able to communicate with you in due course. Meanwhile enquiries are being made through the International Red Cross Committee, and as soon as any definite news is received you will be at once informed.

      If any information regarding your brother is received by you from any source you are requested to be kind enough to communicate it immediately to the Air Ministry.

/The

Mrs. K. Foyster,
  17, Cherry Lane,
    Pitt Street,
      Norwich.

7 More from the Ministry.

      The Air Council desire me to convey to you their sympathy in your present anxiety.

    I am, Madam,

      Your obedient Servant,

Charles Evans

Royal Air Force,

Graveley,

Hunts.

Ref: 35S/C.68/175/P.1.    22nd March, 1945.


Dear Mrs. Foyster,

        I am enclosing a certificate
for the permanent award of the Path Finder Force
Badge, to your Brother, which no doubt you would
like to keep for him.

        I regret I have as yet, no
further news for you.

        Yours sincerely,

        ( H.J.F. Le Good.)
        Wing Commander,
        <u>Squadron Commander.</u>


Mrs. K. Foyster,
17, Cherry Lane,
Pitt Street,
<u>Norwich.</u>

8 The system is unrelenting and stops for no one.

Telephone No:-
COLNBROOK 231/232/233.

In reply please
quote reference:-
CD/FT.64782.

Central Depository,
Royal Air Force,
Colnbrook,
Slough, Bucks.

10th April, 1945.

1813968. W/O. ROE, V. A.

Dear Madam,

The personal effects of the above named as listed
on the attached inventory have been received from the Unit and
are held at the Central Depository in safe custody.

Should you desire these effects to be sent to you
and will kindly return to this office, duly signed and witnessed,
the enclosed form of indemnity, arrangements will be made
accordingly. A prepaid addressed label is enclosed for your
reply.

The item/s shown on the inventory as having been
forwarded to Accounts 13 Department, cannot be released on
indemnity, but will be retained in safe custody during the
"Missing" period.

May I be permitted to express my sympathy with you in
this time of anxiety.

Yours faithfully,

Squadron Leader, Commanding,
Wing Commander, Commanding,
R.A.F. Central Depository.

Mrs.K.Foyster,
17, Cherry Lane,
Pitt Street,
Norwich.

9 Final phase of
the tidying up of an
RAF officer's affairs
starts …

FT64782      PERSONAL EFFECTS OF 1813968 W/O. ROE.V.A.

1 Cardboard carton contg:
1 Despatch case -damaged contg:
 Zipper writing case contg:
 Stamps value 5d                    1 pr. suspenders
 Driving licence                    2 ties
 Private correspondence             1 pr. leather gloves
1 Form 64                           1 pipe
1 Swimming certificate              2 darts
1 tobacco pouch                     3 handkerchiefs
2 torches                           1 swimming suit
1 purse                             4 prs. socks
1 cigarette case                    1 suit pyjamas
1 metal mirror                      2 prs. black leather shoes
1 pocket watch -Chrometre           1 balaclava helmet
1 tin contg:                        1 pullover
 2 wristlet watches                 3 vests
 (1 shockproof                      1 civilian raincoat
  1 No name)                        2 coathangers
Studs
Cuff links
3 Table tennis balls
2 books
Writing paper & envelopes
1 Holy Bible                 NOTE. 1 Post Office Savings Bank Book
2 packs cards                Curtisden No.680,  extracted by Unit
1 clothes brush              and forwarded to Air Ministry, Dept.
1 A.G. brevet                Accts. 13, Worcs.
1 Camera-Brownie
1 tie press
1 leather belt

1 wallet
1 Ever-ready razor

Telephone Nos:
COLNBROOK 231/232/233

In reply please
quote reference:- *FI. 64782*
CD/

Central Depository,
Royal Air Force,
Colnbrook,
Slough, Bucks.

*1-5-45*

<u>1813968 w/o Roe. U.A. (B.X.N.)</u>

Dear Madam,

      In accordance with Air Ministry instructions the personal
effects of the above named as enumerated on the enclosed inventory
have been despatched to you by passenger train.

      When the effects reach you kindly sign and return the
inventory, for which purpose a prepaid addressed label is enclosed
herewith.

      I should like to point out that in the event of the
consignment being received by you showing signs of damage in transit,
you should, in your own interests, mention the fact on any receipt
that you give to the railway company and at the same time perhaps you
will be good enough to notify me in order that the necessary action
can be taken.   Similarly please let me know if the consignment does
not arrive within 14 days from the date of this letter.

Yours faithfully,

*S. Baker*

Wing Commander, Commanding,
<u>R.A.F. Central Depository.</u>

*Mrs. K.L. Foyster.*
*17. Cherry Lane.*
*Pitt Street.*
*Norwich.*

10 ... and continues.

---

No. 35 Squadron,
Royal Air Force,
Graveley,
Hunts.

Ref: 35S/C.68/175/P.1.        7th May, 1945.

Dear Mrs. Foyster,

      Flight Lieutenant Forde, the former
Captain of your Brother's aircraft, has asked me to
pass on to you his sympathy and also that of Flight
Lieutenant Rollins and Flying Officer Carruthers.

      Flight Lieutenant Forde is, of course,
not now on this Squadron but is in Transport Command.

Yours sincerely,

Flight Lieutenant, Adjutant,
for
Wing Commander, Commanding,
<u>No.   35   Squadron.</u>

Mrs. K. Foyster,
17, Cherry Lane,
Pitt Street,
<u>Norwich.</u>

11 Condolences from
his earlier crewmates.

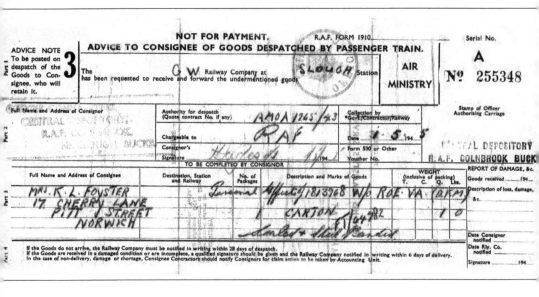

NOT FOR PAYMENT.

R.A.F. FORM 1910

Serial No.

ADVICE TO CONSIGNEE OF GOODS DESPATCHED BY PASSENGER TRAIN.

AIR
MINISTRY

A

Nº 255348

ADVICE NOTE
To be posted on
despatch of the
Goods to Con-
signee, who will
retain it.

**3**

The
has been requested to receive and forward the undermentioned goods

G W Railway Company at SLOUGH Station

Full Name and Address of Consignor

CENTRAL DEPOSITORY,
R.A.F. COLNBROOK
AIR ... ... BUCKS

| Authority for despatch (Quote contract No. if any) | AMOA 1265/43 | Collection by *Govt./Contractor/Railway | Stamp of Officer Authorising Carriage |
| Chargeable to | RAF | Date 1 5 194 5 | |
| Consignor's Signature | Hayles H | Form 530 or Other Voucher No. | ... AL DEPOSITORY R.A.F. COLNBROOK BUCK |

TO BE COMPLETED BY CONSIGNOR

| Full Name and Address of Consignee | Destination, Station and Railway | No. of Packages | Description and Marks of Goods | WEIGHT (inclusive of packing) T. C. Q. Lbs. | REPORT OF DAMAGE, &c. |
|---|---|---|---|---|---|
| MRS. R. L. FOYSTER 17 CHERRY LANE PITT STREET NORWICH | Personal | | Affects 1813768 W/o ROE VA. D.F.M | | Goods received ... 194 Description of loss, damage, &c. |
| | | 1 | CARTON 164 782 | 1 0 | |
| | | | Sealed & steel banded | | |

If the Goods do not arrive, the Railway Company must be notified in writing within 28 days of despatch.
If the Goods are received in a damaged condition or are incomplete, a qualified signature should be given and the Railway Company notified in writing within 6 days of delivery.
In the case of non-delivery, damage or shortage, Consignee Contractors should notify Consignors for claim action to be taken by Accounting Unit.

| Date Consignor notified |
| Date Rly. Co. notified |
| Signature ... 194 |

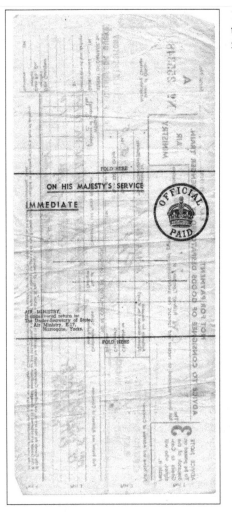

12 The documents of the shipment transferring Victor's possessions to his family, and the outer cover of the form.

GX/CA/202/213/P.3.

R.A.F. Station,
Graveley,
HUNTS.

6th June, 1945.

Dear Mrs. K. Foyster,

With reference to my letter to you of the
31st May, I have since received a further offer of £17/-/-d for
your brother's car which I have accepted on your behalf.

I enclose herewith cheque for this amount
made payable to yourself, also receipt in duplicate. Please
return both copies of receipt to me if this offer is acceptable
to you, and sign over the twopenny stamp.

Yours sincerely,

hw Kitchen F/L

For Group Captain, Commanding,
R.A.F. Station, Graveley.

Mrs. K. Foyster,
17, Cherry Lane,
Pitt Street,
Norwich.

13 The letter relating to the sale of Victor's car.

F/Lt. J.H.Rollins D.F.C.,
207. Magdalen Rd.,
London S.W.I8.
Wednesday 19th., June 46.,

Dear Mrs. Foyster,

     Maybe first of all I should introduce myself, as Vic. may not have mentioned my name. I had the privilege of serving in the same crew as Vic. in the capacity of navigator. We two together with three others remained together throughout, both in Bomber Command and Pathfinder Force. A truly great team, I can say in all modesty.

     Shortly after we broke up on September 1943, I was posted overseas, and have only just returned; after a very exciting tour of duty in India, Burma and China. Last week I went up to the Air Ministry to receive my own award, and it was only then that I learned of your address, and also the fact that you had been to collect Vic's awards.

     May I congratulate you on Vic's behalf; a great friend and a fine gunner. The remainder of the crew and myself owe our lives

to him on many occasions. I can assure he will never be forgotten by his many friends in Earlsfield, especially my Mother, nor by crew.

     Although we have never had the pleasure of meeting, we should be delighted to see you if you ever find yourself round these parts.

     Yours very sincerely,

*John H.* Rollins

14 Letter from previous crewmember, John Rollins.

Telephone :  Gerrard 9234

Extn .............

Any communications on the
subject of this letter should
be addressed to :—
THE
UNDER SECRETARY
OF STATE,
and the following number
quoted :—  P.430140/5/P4B6

Your Ref. ......................

AIR MINISTRY,

(Casualty Branch),

73-77, OXFORD STREET,

W.I.

27ᵗ November,1945.

Madam,

    I am directed to inform you, with deep regret, that
notwithstanding the registration of personnel and the greater
facilities for search which exist following the cessation of
hostilities in the European Theatre, no evidence of the survival
of your brother, Warrant Officer V.A. Roe, D.F.M, (1813968)
Royal Air Force, has been received in the Department since he was
reported missing.

    In these circumstances, and on the assumption that you
have no information which would indicate that he is alive, his
death has now been presumed, for official purposes, to have
occurred on 6th March,1945.

    I am to conclude with an expression of the Air Ministry's
profound sympathy with you in your bereavement.

      I am, Madam,
      Your obedient Servant,

*N. Shepherd.*

for Director of Personal Services.

Mrs. K.Foyster,
  17,Cherry Lane,
    Pitt Street,
      Norwich.

15 The letter confirming KIA dated November 1945. Over eight months after the crash over Chemnitz and over six months after the war has ended.

TELEPHONE NO :—
COLNBROOK 231/232/233.

In reply please
quote reference :—

CD/FT 64782

Central Depository,
  Royal Air Force,
    Colnbrook,
      Slough,
        Bucks.

24th December, 1945.

1813968 W/O ROE, V.A.

Dear Madam,

    The Committee of Adjustment, composed of myself and
two others, which is being held at this office in accordance
with Air Ministry instructions to deal with the estate of the
above named in so far as the Royal Air Force is concerned,
desires to express deep sympathy with you in your bereavement.

    Monetary matters are not dealt with by the Committee
but by the Air Ministry (Accounts 13 Department), Whittington
Road, Worcester, who will, in due course, send a statement of
the service estate, showing all service credits (e.g. cash
found in effects, pay due etc.) and liabilities and will remit
any balance to the deceased's legal representative. If,
therefore, you have any query in this respect perhaps you will be good
enough to write direct to that department.

      Yours faithfully,

      Wing Commander, Commanding,
      R.A.F. Central Depository.

Mrs. K.L. Foyster,
  17, Cherry Lane,
  Pitt Street,
  Norwich.

16 Further tidying up of an officer's affairs.

Letter 1 (Above left):

Tel. No.
Worcester 3411. Ext.............
Correspondence on the subject of
this letter should be addressed to
THE UNDER-SECRETARY
OF STATE
AIR MINISTRY,
and should quote the reference
PP.34793A/45/Accts.13.
Your ref.............

AIR MINISTRY,

WHITTINGTON ROAD,

WORCESTER.

7th February, 1946.

Madam,

The late Warrant Officer V.A. Roe.

I am directed to return the Air Ministry Form 531 sent
to you for completion and to request that the certificate may
be signed by a Minister of Religion, a Magistrate, or a
responsible person to whom you are well known. It is also
requested that you will be good enough to inform this Department
of the address of the above-named Warrant Officer's mother
or if deceased that date of her death, also the date of death
of his father and the addresses of his brothers and sister.

A prepaid envelope is enclosed for your reply.

I am, Madam,
Your obedient Servant,

*A. Wishbone*

for Director of Accounts.

Mrs. K. Foyster,
17, Cherry Lane,
Pitt Street,
Norwich.

---

Letter 2 (Above right):

TEL.: HOLBORN 3434. Extn...........
Communications relating to this
letter should be addressed to :—
THE UNDER SECRETARY OF STATE
quoting :— A.498700/43/S.7.D.
Your Ref.............

AIR MINISTRY,

LONDON, W.C.2.

2nd March, 1946.

Madam,

I am directed to forward the enclosed note
regarding the presentation of decorations by the
King and to request that you will be good enough
to inform this department whether you wish to
attend at Buckingham Palace to receive from His
Majesty the Distinguished Flying Medal and
Conspicuous Gallantry Medal (Flying) conferred on
your brother the late Warrant Officer Victor A. Roe.

I am, Madam,
Your obedient Servant,

Mrs. V. Foyster,
17, Cherry Lane,
Pitt Street,
Norwich.

---

Letter 3 (Left):

Tel. No.
Holborn 3434. Ext.............
Correspondence on the subject of
this letter should be addressed to
THE UNDER-SECRETARY
OF STATE
AIR MINISTRY,
and should quote the reference
S.7(d)/Investitures.
Your ref.............

AIR MINISTRY,

LONDON, W.C.2.

15th March, 1946.

Madam,

I am directed to refer to your letter
of 10th March, and to inform you that your
request that your husband should be allowed
to accompany you at Buckingham Palace, should
be made when you receive the official summons
to attend from the Central Chancery.

I am, Madam,
Your obedient Servant,

Mrs. R. Foyster,
17 Cherry Lane,
Pitt Street,
Norwich.

---

*Above left:* 17 More official
paperwork, almost one year on.

*Above right:* 18 Notification of
the Medal Award Ceremony at
Buckingham Palace, a year on from
the Chemnitz raid.

*Left:* 19 More...

CENTRAL CHANCERY OF
THE ORDERS OF KNIGHTHOOD,
ST. JAMES'S PALACE, S.W. I

23rd April 1946.

Madam,

I have the honour to inform you that your attendance is required at Buckingham Palace at 10.15 o'clock a.m. (doors open at 9.45 o'clock a.m.) on Tuesday, the 7th May, 1946, in order that you, as next of kin, may receive from The King the Conspicuous Gallantry Medal and the Distinguished Flying Medal awarded to your brother, the late Warrant Officer Victor A. Roe, Royal Air Force Volunteer Reserve.

DRESS: Service Dress, Civil Defence Uniform, Morning Dress or dark Lounge Suit.

You may be accompanied by one relation only, who must be a blood relation of the deceased (children under seven years of age may not attend) and I shall be glad if you will complete the enclosed form and return it to me immediately. Two third class return railway vouchers will be forwarded to you if you so desire, and I shall be glad if you will give the details required on the form enclosed.

This letter should be produced on entering the Palace as no further cards of admission will be issued.

I am, Madam,
Your obedient Servant,

*[signature]*
Brigadier
Secretary

Mrs. R. Foyster.

20 The notes explaining the, what, when, where and how of the awards ceremony at the Palace.

Presentations to next-of-kin

1. Arrangements can be made for the persons recorded as the next-of-kin of those awarded decorations to attend at Buckingham Palace to receive the decoration from the King.

2. It is not possible at present to give any indication of the date of the ceremony at which your attendance could be arranged. Reasonable notice of the date would, however, be given to you.

3. One other person would be allowed to attend with you. This guest must be a blood relative of the officer or airman on whom the decoration was conferred and must be 7 or more years of age.

4. It is not possible to arrange for more than one guest to attend at Buckingham Palace or to arrange for the attendance of children under the age of 7.

5. If you or your guest reside outside London, railway warrants will be provided on request to cover third class return travel between the place of residence and London.

6. If for any reason you do not wish to attend, the decoration will be forwarded to you by post.

Air Ministry (S.1cB)
Adastral House,
Kingsway,
London, W.C.2.

G.78073

Tel. No.
~~XXXXXXXXXXX~~
Sloane 3467

AIR MINISTRY,

~~WHITEHALL~~

~~LONDON, S.W.1.~~

P.430140/45/S.14.Cas./408

2, Seville Street,
Knightsbridge,
S.W.1.

25   June, 1948

Dear Mrs. Foyster,

I am very sorry to have to refer to the loss of your
brother, Warrant Officer V.A. Roe, D.F.M., but you would
wish to know that the Royal Air Force Missing Research and
Enquiry Service operating in the Russian Zone of Germany have
discovered that his aircraft came down at Chemnitz though they
are still without definite information about the burial places
of the crew.

A German woman, Frau Seyfert, living at Chemnitz, has
told our people that the aircraft crashed on an allotment in
Friedrich Engels Street, Chemnitz, on 5th March, 1945. The
crew, she states, were killed. She found the body of the
navigator, Flight Lieutenant K.S.Smith, in a private garden,
with an unopened parachute nearby. There was no doubt as to
identity, as she found Flight Lieutenant Smith's identity card,
which has now been sent to us. Frau Seyfert adds that the
crew were buried in the City Cemetery, Chemnitz.

Frau Seyfert's letter gives us the first definite information
that the aircraft reached its target and that it crashed in
the town. Hitherto we had had no news of its fate. It is
reasonably certain that all seven members of the crew were
killed, and that they were all buried in the City Cemetery.
Until, however, our Search Officers could obtain from the
Russians permission to visit Chemnitz, nothing further could be
discovered.

/When

Mrs. K. Foyster,
17 Cherry Lane,
Pitt Street,
Norwich.

21 Frau Seyfert's information passed on to Victor's family.

When at last a search team visited Chemnitz, it was
found that there were two mass graves in the City Cemetery,
one of 67 Germans and other victims of the raid, the other
of 294.

A limited amount of exhumation was permitted by the
Russians. Ten bodies were disinterred, but only one was
of an airman. He was a flight sergeant wireless operator
of another Lancaster which had crashed at Chemnitz on the
same operation.

We have asked the Russians to let our teams completely
exhume both the mass graves, as that is the only way of
obtaining the information that is so vitally needed. At
least four crews are believed to be buried in these graves:
so far we have been able to identify only one man.

Any further information that we receive will be passed
on to you without delay.

May I again offer you our sympathy in your great loss.

Yours sincerely,

A.P. le M. Sinkinson

( Squadron Leader in Casualty Branch )

# *Victory Message*

To:     The Path Finder Force

From    Air Vice-Marshal D. C. T. Bennett, CB, CBE, DSO

Great Britain and the Commonwealth have made a contribution to the civilised world so magnificent that history alone will be able to appreciate it fully. Through disaster and triumph, sometimes supported and sometimes alone the British races have steadfastly and energetically over many long years flung their forces against international criminals. They have fought the war from end to end without a moment's respite, in all the theatres, and with all the arms, land, sea and air.

Bomber Command share in this great effort has been a major one. You, each one of you, have made that possible. The Path Finder Force has shouldered a grave responsibility. It had lead Bomber Command, the greatest striking force ever known. That we have been successful can be seen in the far-reaching results which the Bomber offensive has achieved. That is the greatest reward that the Path Finder Force ever hopes to receive, for those results have benefited all law-abiding peoples.

Whilst you have been hard at work through these vital years I have not interrupted you with messages of praise and congratulation, as I would like to have done. You were too busy; but now that your great contribution to the world has been made, I want to thank you each man and woman of you personally to congratulate you on your unrelenting spirit and energy and on the results you have achieved.

Happiness to you all—always. Keep Pressing On along the Path of Peace.

DON BENNETT

Headquarters, Path Finder Force
European V-Day, 1945

Issued just a few short weeks after his death, no-one could have deserved their CO's praise more than Victor.

# Victor Roe Combat Operations

| Date | Aircraft | Serial | Pilot | Target | Target type | Notes |
|---|---|---|---|---|---|---|
| 22.08.43 | Wellington X | LN443 | Forde | In Dutch Waters | | Laying Mines. Used Gee |
| 23.08.43 | Wellington X | LN442 | Forde | Terschelling | | Laying Mines. Used Gee |
| 24.08.43 | Wellington X | LN443 | Forde | Spiekeroog | | Laying Mines. Used visual contact |
| 26.08.43 | Wellington X | LN443 | Forde | Isle de Croix | | Laying Mines. Used visual contact |
| 27.08.43 | Wellington X | LN443 | Forde | Ils d'Oleron | | Laying Mines. |
| 30.08.43 | Wellington X | LN442 | Forde | Möncheng'bach | | Bombing from 18,000ft. Target time 02.14 on 31.04 |
| 31.08.43 | Wellington X | LN442 | Forde | Undisclosed | | Bomb Sight faliure. RTB |
| 20.12.43 | Halifax III | HX266 | Forde | Frankfurt | | Bombing from 17,000ft. Used green PFF flares |
| 29.12.43 | Halifax III | HX274 | Forde | Undisclosed | | Bombing from 22,000ft. Used row of PPFF flares |
| 20.01.44 | Halifax III | HX266 | Forde | Berlin | | Bombing from 19,000ft. Used PFF red sky markers |
| 21.01.44 | Halifax III | HX266 | Forde | Magdaburg | | Bombing from 20,000ft. Used PFF green TIs. Flack damage (slight) over Wilhelmshaven |
| 24.02.44 | Halifax III | LV837 | Forde | Schweinfurt | Ball Bearing plant | Bombing from 20,000ft. Used PFF red TIs. |
| | | | | | | Precautionary landing Tangmere. Fuel shortage |
| 06.03.44 | Halifax III | LV826 | Forde | Trappes | | Bombing from 15,00ft. Used red TIs. and visual |
| 07.03.44 | Halifax III | LV826 | Forde | Le Mans | | Target obscured. No TIs seen. Load jettisoned RTB |
| 26/27.04.44 | Lancaster | ND731 (A) | Forde | Essen | Railway Yards | PFF Bombing Supporter |
| 30/01.04/05.44 | Lancaster | ND762 (E) | Forde | Acheres | Railway Yards | PFF Bombing Supporter |
| 03/04.05.44 | Lancaster | ND762 (E) | Forde | Montedidier | Airfield | PFF Bombing Supporter |
| 06/07.05.44 | Lancaster | ND762 (E) | Forde | Nantes | Railway Yards | PFF Bombing Supporter |
| 08/09.05.44 | Lancaster | ND929 (J) | Forde | Haine-St-Pierre | Railway Yards | PFF Bombing Main Force   Awarded DFM for his work |

| Date | Aircraft | Serial | Pilot | Target | Type | Role |
|---|---|---|---|---|---|---|
| 11/12.05.44 | Lancaster | ND690 (C) | Forde | Louvain | Railway Yards | PFF Bombing Supporter |
| 21/22.05.44 | Lancaster | ND693 (H) | Forde | Duisburg | Industrial | PFF Bombing Supporter |
| 22/23.05.44 | Lancaster | ND755 (B) | Forde | Dortmund | Railway Yards | PFF Bombing Supporter |
| 24/25.05.44 | Lancaster | ND916 (F) | Forde | Aachen | Railway Yards | PFF Bombing Supporter |
| 27/28.05.44 | Lancaster | ND916 (F) | Forde | Bourg Leopold | Military Camp | PFF Bombing Illuminator |
| 28/29.05.44 | Lancaster | ND916 (F) | Forde | Mardyck | Gun Emplacements | PFF Bombing Bomber |
| 07/08.06.44 | Lancaster | ND916 (F) | Forde | Foret-de-Cerisy | D-Day Support | PFF Bombing Bomber |
| 08/09.06.44 | Lancaster | ND696 (E) | Forde | Fougeres | Railway Yards | PFF Bombing Bomber |
| 09/10.06.44 | Lancaster | ND692 (F) | Forde | Rennes | Airfield | PFF Bombing Bomber |
| 15/16.06.44 | Lancaster | ND936 (C) | Forde | Lens | Railway Yards | PFF Bombing Bomber/ |
| 16/17.06.44 | Lancaster | ND916 (F) | Forde | Sterkrade | Oil Plant | PFF Bombing Visual Backer-up |
| 22/23.06.44 | Lancaster | ND936 (C) | Forde | Laon | Rail Yards | PFF Bombing Illuminator |
| 24/25.06.44 | Lancaster | ND929 (J) | Forde | Middel-Straete | VI Site | PFF Bombing Bomber |
| 27/28.06.44 | Lancaster | ND929 (L) | Forde | Oisemont | VI Site | PFF Bombing Bomber |
| 02.07.44 | Lancaster | ND702 (E) | Forde | Oisemont | VI Site | PFF Bombing Deputy Master Bomber |
| 04.07.44 | Lancaster | ND702 (G) | Forde | Villeneuve St G | Railway Yards | PFF Bombing Illuminator |
| 06.07.44 | Lancaster | ND690 (O) | Forde | Marquise | V3 Site | PFF Bombing Deputy Master Bomber |
| 07/08.7.44 | Lancaster | ND646 (U) | Bryant | Caen | VI Site | PFF Bombing Deputy Master Bomber |
| 09.07.44 | Lancaster | ND702 (G) | Forde | Catelliers | VI Site | PFF Bombing Deputy Master Bomber |
| 10.07.44 | Lancaster | ND702 (G) | Forde | Nucourt | VI Site | PFF Bombing Bomber |
| 12.07.44 | Lancaster | ND702 (G) | Forde | Rollez | VI Site | PFF Bombing Bomber |
| 15.07.44 | Lancaster | PB123 (F) | Forde | Les Lande | VI Site | PFF Bombing Deputy Master Bomber |
| 16.07.44 | Lancaster | ND702 (G) | Forde | St Philbert | VI Site | PFF Bombing Bomber |
| 31.7/01.8.44 | Lancaster | ND702 (G) | Forde | Foret de Nippe | VI Site | PFF Bombing Master Bomber |
| 03.08.44 | Lancaster | ND702 (G) | Forde | Bois de Casson | VI Site | PFF Bombing Backer-up |
| 04.08.44 | Lancaster | ND702 (G) | Forde | Bec-d'Ambes | Oil Plant | PFF Bombing Deputy Master Bomber |
| 06.08.44 | Lancaster | ND702 (G) | Forde | Foret de Nippe | VI Site | PFF Bombing Deputy Master Bomber |

| Date | Aircraft | Serial | Pilot | Target | Target Type | Role | Notes |
|---|---|---|---|---|---|---|---|
| 07/08.08.44 | Lancaster | ND702 (G) | Forde | Totallize | Army Support | PFF Bombing Backer-up | |
| 09/10.08.44 | Lancaster | ND702 (G) | Forde | Foret de Nippe | VI Site | PFF Bombing Master Bomber | |
| 11.08.44 | Lancaster | ND702 (G) | Forde | Douai | Railway Yards | PFF Bombing Master Bomber | |
| 12/13.08.44 | Lancaster | ND702 (G) | Forde | Russelsheim | Motor Works | PFF Bombing Primary Visual Marker | |
| 14 08.44 | Lancaster | ND702 (G) | Forde | Falaise AP24 | Army Support | PFF Bombing Master Bomber | |
| 15.08.44 | Lancaster | PB257 (C) | Forde | Le Culot | VI Site / Airfield | PFF Bombing Master Bomber | |
| 16/17.08.44 | Lancaster | ND646 (U) | Forde | Stettin | Port | PFF Bombing Visual Centre | Landed at Foulsham |
| 18/19.08.44 | Lancaster | ND702 (G) | Forde | Bremen | Port / Industrial | PFF Bombing Primary Visual Marker | |
| 31.08.44 | Lancaster | ND702 (G) | Forde | Pourchinte | VI Site | PFF Bombing Master Bomber | |
| 05.09.44 | Lancaster | ND702 (G) | Forde | Le Havre | Army Support | PFF Bombing Backer-up | |
| 06.09.44 | Lancaster | ND702 (G) | Forde | Le Havre AP4 | Army Support | PFF Bombing Backer-up | |
| 08.09.44 | Lancaster | ND702 (G) | Forde | Le Havre AP15 | Army Support | PFF Bombing Backer-up | |
| 09.09.44 | Lancaster | ND702 (G) | Forde | Le Havre AP7 | Army Support | PFF Bombing Master Bomber | |
| 10.09.44 | Lancaster | ND702 (G) | Forde | Le Havre BUIK2 | Army Support | PFF Bombing Master Bomber | |
| 27.09.44 | Lancaster | ND907 (G) | Forde | Calais AP14 | Army Support | PFF Bombing Master Bomber | |
| 28.09.44 | Lancaster | ND907 (G) | Forde | Calais AP18 | Army Support | PFF Bombing Master Bomber | |
| 05.10.44 | Lancaster | ND907 (G) | Forde | Saarbrucken | Railway Yards | PFF Bombing Primary Marker | |
| 11.10.44 | Lancaster | ND907 (G) | Forde | Fort Frederik | Gun Battery | PFF Bombing Master Bomber | |
| 14.15.10.44 | Lancaster | ND907 (G) | Watson | Duisberg | 1st Wave | PFF Bombing Supporter | |
| 02.11.44 | Lancaster | ND907 (G) | Watson | Dusseldorf | Industry | PFF Bombing Supporter | |
| 04/05.11.44 | Lancaster | PB288 (R ) | Watson | Bochum | Steel Plant | PFF Bombing Supporter | |
| 06.11.44 | Lancaster | ND916 (K) | Watson | Gelesenkirchen | Oil Plant | PFF Bombing Supporter | |
| 27.11.44 | Lancaster | PB257 (T) | Watson | Freiburg | Various | PFF Bombing Blind Illuminator | |
| 29.11.44 | Lancaster | PB343 (N) | Watson | Dortmund | City | PFF Bombing Blind Secondary Marker | |
| 04.12.44 | Lancaster | ME355 (O) | Watson | Heimbach | Dam | PFF Bombing Supporter | |
| 05.12.44 | Lancaster | ME335 (O) | Watson | Soest | Railway Yards | PFF Bombing Supporter | |
| 06/07.12.44 | Lancaster | ME335 (O) | Watson | Mersburg | Oil | PFF Bombing Blind illuminator | |

| Date | Aircraft | Code | Pilot | Target | Type | Role | Remarks |
|---|---|---|---|---|---|---|---|
| 15/16.12.44 | Lancaster | ME355 (O) | Watson | Ludwigshaven | Oil | PFF Bombing Supporter | |
| 17/18.12.44 | Lancaster | ME355 (O) | Watson | Ulm | Bunker / Vehicles | PFF Bombing Blind illuminator | |
| 22/23.12.44 | Lancaster | ME355 (O) | Watson | Koblenz | Transport | PFF Bombing Blind Secondary Marker | |
| 24/25.12.44 | Lancaster | ME335 (O) | Osmond | Nippes | Rail Yards | PFF Bombing Supporter | |
| 28/29.12.44 | Lancaster | ME335 (O) | Watson | Gelesenkirchen | Oil | PFF Bombing Supporter | |
| 02/03.01.45 | Lancaster | ME333 (S) | Watson | Ludwigshaven | Oil | PFF Bombing Blind Secondary Marker | |
| 05/06.01.45 | Lancaster | ME335 (O) | Watson | Hanover | City | PFF Bombing Blind Secondary Marker | |
| 06/07.01.45 | Lancaster | ND676 (E) | Watson | Hanau | Railway Yards | PFF Bombing Blind Secondary Marker | |
| 07/08.01.45 | Lancaster | ME335 (O) | Watson | Munich | City / Industry | PFF Bombing Blind Secondary Marker | |
| 13/14.01.45 | Lancaster | ME335 (O) | Watson | Saarbrucken | Railways | PFF Bombing Blind Secondary Marker | Landed Tangmere |
| 14/15.01.45 | Lancaster | PB288 (U) | Watson | Mersburg-Leuna | Oil Plant | PFF Bombing Blind Marker | Landed Exeter |
| 16/17.01.45 | Lancaster | PB288 (U) | Watson | Zeitz | Oil Plant | PFF Bombing Blind Marker | |
| 28/29.01.45 | Lancaster | ME333 (S) | Watson | Stuttgart | Rail Yards | PFF Bombing Blind Secondary Marker | |
| 01/02.02.45 | Lancaster | PB305 (P) | Watson | Mainz | Industry | PFF Bombing Blind Secondary Marker | |
| 04/05.02.45 | Lancaster | ME333 (S) | Watson | Bonn | City | PFF Bombing Blind Secondary Marker | |
| 07/08.02.45 | Lancaster | ME333 (S) | Watson | Goch | Army Support /Town | PFF Bombing Blind illuminator | |
| 08/09.02.45 | Lancaster | ME333 (S) | Watson | Politz | Oil Plant | PFF Bombing Blind Secondary Marker | |
| 13/14.02.45 | Lancaster | ME333 (S) | Watson | Dresden | City | PFF Bombing Operation Thunderclap | |
| 14/15.02.45 | Lancaster | ME333 (S) | Watson | Chemnitz | Railway Yards | PFF Bombing Operation Thunderclap | |
| 20/21.02.45 | Lancaster | ME333 (S) | Watson | Dortmund | City | PFF Bombing Blind Secondary Marker | |
| 21/22.02.45 | Lancaster | ME333 (S) | Watson | Duisburg | City / Various | PFF Bombing Blind Secondary Marker | |
| 23.02.45 | Lancaster | ME333 (S) | Watson | Essen | City / Various | PFF Bombing Blind Secondary Marker | |
| 27.02.45 | Lancaster | ME333 (S) | Watson | Mainz | Industry | PFF Bombing Blind Secondary Marker | |
| 01.03.45 | Lancaster | PB305 (P) | Watson | Mannheim | Industry | PFF Bombing Blind Secondary Marker | |
| 05/06.03.45 | Lancaster | ME333 (S) | Watson | Chemnitz | Railway Yards | PFF Bombing Blind Secondary Marker | Failed to Return |

Awarded CGM notification arrived posthumiously

APPENDIX 2

# Victor's Family Tree

**Edward Clifton ROE**
b Norwich XX.11.1906 Worlds End Lane.
m July 1927 Phyllis Tomlinson in Derbyshire
d 13.11.1954 Chesterfield Derbyshire
Coalminer

**Albert Blythe ROE**
b Norwich 22.08.1908 Burrels Yard. Colegate St.
d 1966 Camarthen Wales

**Kate Laura ROE**
b Norwich 15.12.1910 Prince of Wales Yd., St Benedict St.
m Feb 1944 Ernest A. Foyster in Norwich
d 24.12.1982 Norwich Norfolk

**Bertie Alfred ROE**
b Norwich 21.04.1913 Stonemasons Sq., St Georges Street.
m Q4 1935 Adeline H. Morris in Poplar
d Q1 1986 Taunton Somerset
Farmer

**George Arthur ROE**
b Norwich 21.02.1916 The Lodge Bowthorpe St.
d Q3 1916 Norwich Norfolk

**Gladys Violet ROE**
b Norwich 29.07.1917 The Lodge Bowthorpe St.
m April 1961 John Roche in Sidney
d Circa 1998 Sydney Australia

**Wilfred ROE**
b Norwich 26.05.1920 The Lodge Bowthorpe St.
m Q4 1956 Margaret R. Fowler in Luton
d Q3 1996 Luton Bedfordshire
Soldier and Storekeeper

**Victor Arthur ROE**
b Norwich 24.05.1923 The Lodge Bowthorpe St.
d 06.03.1945 Chemnitz Germany
Air Crew RAF

**Kathleen Lily ROE**
b Norwich 09.09.1926 The Lodge Bowthorpe St.
m Q2 1958 Oswald G. Weller in Norwich

# Bibliography

Bennett, Don C. T., *Pathfinder*, (Goodall, 1958)
Bodle, Peter FRAeS and Boulter, Eddie, *Mosquito to Berlin*, (Pen & Sword, 2007)
Cooper, Alan W., *Bravery Awards for Aerial Combat*, (Pen & Sword, 2007)
Coverdale, Christopher, *Pathfinders 635 Squadron*, (Self Published, 2009)
Sharp, Syd, *Black Boots & Short Trousers*, (Self Published, 1995)
Smith, Ron, DFM, *Rear Gunner Pathfinders*, (Goodall/Crecy 1987)
Stocker, Flt Lt Ted, *A Pathfinder's War*, (Grub Street, 2009)

# Index